Social Skills
Training
and the
Professional
Helper

JOHN AND
MARY COLLINS

Social Skills Training and the Professional Helper

JOHN WILEY & SONS
Chichester · New York · Brisbane · Toronto · Singapore

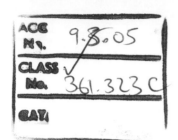

Copyright © 1992 by John Wiley & Sons Ltd,
Baffins Lane, Chichester,
West Sussex PO19 1UD, England

Other Wiley Editorial Offices

John Wiley & Sons, Inc., 605 Third Avenue,
New York, NY 10158-0012, USA

Jacaranda Wiley Ltd, G.P.O. Box 859, Brisbane,
Queensland 4001, Australia

John Wiley & Sons (Canada) Ltd, 22 Worcester Road,
Rexdale, Ontario M9W 1L1, Canada

John Wiley & Sons (SEA) Pte Ltd, 37 Jalan Pemimpin # 05-04,
Block B, Union Industrial Building, Singapore 2057

Library of Congress Cataloging-in-Publication Data:

Collins, John, *1929–*
    Social skills training and the professional helper / John and
Mary Collins.
        p.   cm.
    Includes bibliographical references and index.
    ISBN 0-471-93145-4
    1. Social skills—Study and teaching.   2. Interpersonal relations—
Study and teaching.   I. Collins, Mary, *1931–* .   II. Title.
HM299.C64   1992   91–29939
    361.3′2—dc20   CIP

British Library Cataloguing in Publication Data:

A catalogue record for this book is available
from the British Library.

ISBN 0-471-93145-4

Typeset in 11/13 pt Photina by Alden Multimedia Ltd, Northampton
Printed and bound in Great Britain by Biddles Ltd, Guildford and King's Lynn

Dedicated to our younger generation:
Chris and Sue, and their cousins Terry and Ray

CONTENTS

PREFACE

This is a book about how people interact and about the ways in which they can improve that interaction so that it serves them better. We do not have to be paragons ourselves in order to help people in this way, but we do have to reflect on our own interaction with others and make use of learning opportunities to interact better with them so that what we do and say expresses better what we intend and is more helpful to them. Hence this book will explore ways in which professional helpers may tackle some of the interpersonal difficulties which they may encounter, as well as describing social skills training methods for use with clients. These methods are essentially the same, though they will have to be adapted in detail to suit the particular characteristics of different client groups. As with other methods of helping like psychotherapy and counselling, the progress which we make in developing our understanding of ourselves and our skills in interaction is closely linked to our effectiveness in helping others.

The authors' background is mainly in social work practice and education, a fact which is reflected in the literature on which we draw and, to a lesser extent, in the material used to illustrate problems encountered and methods of working. It will be found, however, that this material has a very wide application to professional practice. Probation officers, psychologists, community psychiatric nurses, occupational therapists, youth and community workers, counsellors, teachers, and especially staff working in residential and day care settings—all are likely to find these subjects familiar, and as the different professions work increasingly together we shall be more able to share and benefit from each other's experience and skills.

In order therefore to make the content accessible to the widest possible readership (in America as well as Britain), we have tried to avoid the use of jargon and technical terms. In the field of handicap, we have used old-established terms familiar in the USA and elsewhere in Europe (for instance "mental handicap", rather than the recently introduced "learning difficulties", a decision discussed more fully at the start of Chapter 12). We hope that readers will be able to recognize most of the problems which we identify and to use, in their own individual ways, what the students and practitioners who have worked with us have achieved by their honesty, their commitment to professional values, their use of discipline and structure and their creative, imaginative approaches.

ACKNOWLEDGEMENTS

We are grateful to Jean Packman and Bill Jordan, colleagues at Exeter University, for their sympathetic consideration and constructive criticisms of earlier drafts of this book; also to Vi Stevenson for secretarial help in the preparation of these drafts. For much of the material, we are indebted to successive groups of students with whom we have worked. Many of the situations, difficulties and strategies described here have been shared with us by students following the social work courses at Exeter University. Our thanks are due to them, and to students following in-service training on the South-West Peninsula Certificate in Social Service Scheme while practising in residential and day care settings, whose contribution has also been invaluable—sensitive, creative and innovative. The work which all these students have done with us has seemed to assume greater significance and to achieve higher standards as the years have passed, and has contributed to the general evolution in British social work training during this period, leading to the present Diploma in Social Work courses and to the central position properly accorded in them to the development of practice skills.

SECTION I

Social skills and how they may be learned and evaluated

This section is concerned with social skills training in general, whether for helpers or for clients. It begins by exploring the nature of social skills training and the way in which it relates to the helping process in general, and proceeds to consider the subject of assessment as the foundation for all such training.

CHAPTER 1

The relationship of social skills training to the traditional concerns of the helping professions

The activity of helping others through personal contact and inter-action to resolve problems of living has a long and honourable history. Social work has been one such activity ever since its origins in the concern to help people, particularly at times of crisis and distress, but there are also many other professions whose concerns and fields of activity may overlap with it. They include professionals with other, more specialized skills, but also many trained and highly skilled people who work on a voluntary basis. All these will have an interest in what has always been a central social work concern: the quality of the interaction between individuals and their environment. For all of them, the nature of the interaction between the worker and the person being helped is seen as a crucial element in the helping process. This book deals with both kinds of interaction; indeed it is based on the assumption that there is no essential difference between the problems of social performance experienced by clients and by their helpers. Social skills training also has a long history—longer than is commonly supposed, going back to the art of rhetoric as first practised in Athens in the fifth century BC. Its aim is to help people to develop ways of interacting with others which are both closer to their own intentions and likely to lead to greater satisfaction in their social relationships.

Much of the practice of the various forms of psychotherapy and counselling, as well as much of the training of professional helpers, would no doubt be seen as embodying similar aims. The distinguishing features of a social skills approach, however, are the following:

- Precise identification of the situations in which difficulty is experienced and skills are to be practised

- Rehearsal of the piece of behaviour in question, with feedback including comments, discussion and suggestions for any modification
- The possibility of a change in the way participants behave, or at least an increase in the range of options they have for future behaviour

An approach so clearly based on an explicit commitment to producing a change in the way people behave would quite obviously not be relevant to many situations encountered in professional helping, as (for instance) where the focus was on the provision of material aid or on providing support through a period of acute emotional distress. In many others, however, such an approach could be most productive: an adolescent in conflict with his parents, his teachers or his peers could learn ways of presenting himself less aggressively; the parent of a disruptive child can learn to be more assertive in controlling him (or her); a claimant who gets into frequent confrontations with welfare benefits staff can develop an assertive style of interaction in place of his previous alternation between passivity and aggressiveness.

Our formulation of the central features of social skills work clearly locates it within the general context of interpersonal helping and indeed within the traditional boundaries of social work. Most of the published material on the subject, however, emanates from psychologists and seems designed for use in specifically clinical settings. It relies heavily on statistical method, and it is not easy for people from other disciplines to deduce what application it might have to their own work. Our intention in the present book is to describe for a variety of workers in field, day care and residential settings a practical method of working which is highly flexible and adaptable to different client groups and life situations and which can be understood without exhaustive study of psychological theory and statistical method.

It has been stressed that problems of social performance, far from being peculiar to clients, are part of the common lot of humanity. Hence there can be no question of workers seeing themselves as totally competent and beyond any possibility of criticism. Indeed, because the way they present themselves to others is so important to their professional effectiveness and because they frequently find themselves in highly stressful situations, social skills training is a most useful component of any course of training for professional helpers.

A major aim (though not of course the sole aim) of professional training must be the development of professional skills, among which interpersonal skills clearly figure prominently. As Rackham and his colleagues (1971) stress, "a skill can be acquired only through practice: an interactive skill is no exception". You would not expect to learn to play the piano or drive a car (or to do either of these things better) by reading a book or attending a lecture sequence. Nor will practice alone necessarily produce an accomplished performance; you may simply go on making the same mistakes unless you can also obtain accurate feedback on the quality of what you do. It is for this reason that even the most outstanding musicians continue to listen to recordings of their own performances and to take lessons. Without feedback of this kind skills will not continue to improve; there is even evidence that they may deteriorate. Thus studies such as that by Wynne et al (1987) have shown that the resuscitation skills of nursing staff actually diminish after completion of training if they receive no feedback on what they are doing. Evidence such as this seems to make a case not only for interpersonal skills training as part of a professional qualifying course but also as a recurrent input in the form of refresher courses.

Developing these professional skills may be seen as a specialized form of social skills training, an extension of a general method into a specific, limited area. In a very real sense, however, it is logical to consider the subject of professional skills training first, since you need to have worked on and developed your own interpersonal skills in order to be effective in helping others with theirs. Running social skills groups for clients requires in the leader a very wide range of skills. The existing social skills literature does not help much with this; it tells group leaders what they should do without much indication of the skills they need to do it. In fact, the interpersonal skills which are needed for this kind of work are a combination of many of the practice skills involved in other methods of professional helping; it is only the combination that is novel. It seems logical, therefore, for us to consider the worker skills described in Section II before going on in Section III to methods of helping clients develop their skills. In this first part, however, our starting point will be those considerations which apply equally to interpersonal skill development in workers and clients.

Skills Training and the Social Work Tradition

The definition of social skills training in terms of improvement in the quality of interaction between individuals clearly locates it within the scope of traditional social work. This can be illustrated by definitions of the aims of social casework such as that of Hollis (1956), who states that the method "endeavours to enable the individual to meet his needs more fully and to function more adequately in his social relationships". The social skills approach would not have seemed strange to such pioneers of early work with the socially disadvantaged as Elizabeth Fry and Octavia Hill, for whom it was always a principal aim to leave people more capable than when they first met them of coping with the demands of social living.

It is recorded of Josephine Butler that on her first visit to the Liverpool Workhouse she sat down on the stone floor of the cellar with the bedraggled, destitute (and no doubt noisy, quarrelsome and foul-mouthed) girls to pick oakum with them and joined in their laughter at her own feeble efforts. Before leaving, she asked if someone would learn some verses from the Bible before her return, and found when she next came that one girl was able to stand and recite her favourite verses to the others. A far cry from a modern skills group, it may be thought, and yet the central elements are the same: enter into people's immediate concerns as far as you can, don't be afraid to make a fool of yourself, give them something to do between meetings, keep it simple and within their capabilities, and promote recognition of their achievement by other members of the group. At the other historical extreme from this nineteenth-century initiative, the Barclay Committee (1982) defined social work counselling as a process "through which clients are *helped to change* (our emphasis) or to tolerate some aspects of themselves or their environment".

A concern with ethical values has always characterized writing about social work, and any method of practice which conflicts with the values traditionally held as of central importance would need to justify itself. This is not, however, the case with social skills training, which can be shown to exemplify these central values. While there are many formulations of social work values, that of Butrym (1976) is particularly simple and comprehensive, and hence the most convenient to cite here. She posits three central values: respect for persons, belief in the social nature of man, and belief in the possibility of change and growth. Social skills training expresses respect for individuals by offering them the possibility of a more satisfying quality of experience, by involving them in changing their own lives and in most cases by making them the arbiters of what they want to achieve. Its commitment to the other two principles of concern with the quality of human interaction and the individual's potential for positive change is even more explicit.

Insight and Behavioural Change

While it seems clear then that social skills training falls within the general domain of professional helping, we do not present it as a total answer to the kinds of problems with which helpers are concerned. Indeed, it can often only be commenced when the work with the clients in question has been in progress for some time and they have reached the point where they are ready to undertake it. They have to believe that some change is realistically possible and that they will derive some benefit from it; they also have to recognize that they have specific problems in the way in which they interact with other people and be prepared to work on it. None of this is easy: the recognition that a pattern of social relationships characterized by the individual's being ignored, isolated, exploited or involved in arguments or even fights has something to do with the way that individual presents himself or herself to other people requires a degree of self-awareness and insight into the effects of one's own conduct upon others. It may take some time for this to develop, so that the earlier stages of work with a given client may need to take the form of exploration and counselling—whether this be done by another worker or the one who is to provide the social skills training. Moreover, the training itself is not purely behavioural but needs to take account of the way people think about themselves, as well as the way in which they behave.

Many approaches to interpersonal helping have traditionally

accorded a central importance to the development of insight in the client. This has been seen as the essential precursor of any durable behavioural change, hence any purely behavioural method of achieving change in interaction with others would be a mechanical and superficial phenomenon, an argument which will be discussed shortly. Approaches based solely on the development of insight assume that it is essential for individuals to understand *why* they behave as they do before they will be able to behave differently; this knowledge has usually been concerned with the relationship between early history and present behaviour, as interpreted in the light of one of the various psychodynamic schools such as those of Freud, Klein and Bowlby. Once clients have gained this understanding it is assumed that they will thereby be enabled to change their behaviour in any way that may be required to enable them to get more satisfaction out of their interaction with others.

There are two problems about this approach in its simple form. One is that we cannot really claim to know why people behave in ways that are self-defeating. There are a number of competing theories about how such patterns develop and no satisfactory evidence to enable us to choose between them. The second problem is that the approach fails to consider *how* people learn specific kinds of social behaviour and whether the desired behaviour actually falls within their repertoire.

A concept of insight as a process of becoming aware of emotional factors in psychological functioning, some of which may be unconscious or partly conscious, does not represent the use of the term which would seem most valuable for our present purpose. Yelloly, in her discussion of the relationship of insight to behavioural change (Jehu et al 1972), draws attention to three different senses in which the term is used. The first of these is that attached to it in general parlance, in which it is almost synonymous with "understanding" in depth. The second sense relates to the psychoanalytic use of the term discussed above. Between these two meanings, however, there is a third sense: the term is used to designate awareness of one's own emotions, their role in one's behaviour and the effect which this may have upon others. Here, certainly, is a concept which is clearly of great significance for social skills training. Yelloly concludes her discussion: ". . . the kind of cognitive insight which is related to problem-solving in the here-and-now appears to play an important role in actual casework practice, though it has been sadly neglected in theoretical accounts. Since the knowledge of social work must relate to professional practice, it is important that the concept of psychological insight should not be understood in an exclusively psycho-dynamic sense but should be expanded to include those more cognitive aspects discussed above".

In this sense then, some degree of insight must be viewed as an essential prerequisite to effective social skills work, and if this topic is not given further discussion in these pages it is because we have taken this as our starting-point. However, it cannot be seen as more than a prerequisite: the insight in itself will not enable anyone to practise skills which have never been learned. At this stage, the *opportunity* to learn is what is needed, and it is above all with the provision of learning opportunities that this book is concerned. Before going on to discuss and illustrate the right kinds of learning opportunities, both for clients and for workers in training, it seems important to conclude this chapter with some of the objections which have been raised against this method of intervention.

The first objection, namely that the approach involves imposing our own views of how people should behave on clients, whom we manipulate into conforming with them, requires careful consideration. The method is indeed a highly directive one and involves workers in giving clients very clear instructions about what to do. Hence it is essential that careful preparatory work is done to ensure that there is a full and free agreement at the outset about the objectives and the methods to be used to attain them. This objection, then, is a real one, but its force can be overcome given sufficient attention to preparation. A less telling objection lies in the assertion that social skills training, like other behavioural approaches, only "treats symptoms", leaving a presumed underlying cause un-touched. An explicit analogy with disease is sometimes put forward, the behaviour problem (or deficit) being likened to the rash which testifies to the presence of measles. One reply to this argument is to say that since we cannot actually cure measles it makes sense to put calamine on the spots, for symptom relief is a perfectly respect-able therapeutic procedure, but it may be added, more conclusively, that in most cases no-one can be sure that there *is* any underlying disease. Indeed, since problems of social performance are such a common experience, it seems excessive to regard anxiety about dealing with powerful officials or making new acquaintances as evidence of pathology, any more than we would in the case of anxiety about public speaking or unwillingness to complain of poor service in a restaurant. We cannot in this context divide people into the healthy and the sick; there is a whole continuum of social competence, and a complex one at that, since in any group some members will be more inhibited in one situation but others will be competent in this field and less so in another.

It may also be objected that the method is mechanistic and turns out carbon copies of some model (rather than enabling people to express their individual personalities), or that it is condescending in its assumption of superior competence in the worker, and even more so in the giving of praise to clients for performances which objectively must be seen as of low standard. Such objections seem more substantial in theory than they prove in practice, for a sensitive worker will readily appreciate the real achievement which even a mediocre performance represents for a very inhibited client, and will also be struck by the way that each client in a group does in fact produce a version which is truly her or his own, not a mere slavish copy of some model which has been offered. Meichenbaum (1977) makes the same point:

> . . . the modelling or observational learning that is taking place should *not* be equated with mimicry, exact topographical matching, or superficial imitation.

There is a more general accusation which has been levelled at all forms of individual and most forms of group work, namely that it concentrates attention upon individual shortcomings and tends to reconcile people to a social system which is intrinsically unjust, and hence itself constitutes the appropriate target for intervention. Social skills training cannot altogether be defended against such a charge and perhaps it does not need to be, since the people we are trying to help have problems which are too urgent to wait for a solution at national level which may be long delayed. Some problems, moreover, like those of making friends, are not amenable to government action, and it can justifiably be said in favour of social skills training that it may be used to enable people to *challenge* unresponsive bureaucracy and arbitrary authority, rather than simply accepting them.

CHAPTER 2   The practicalities of skills training

It is a central assumption of the present approach to the development of skills in personal interaction, be they general or specialized, that social behaviour is *learned*: in other words, that the way people behave to each other is not the straightforward, uncomplicated outcome of their needs and emotions but is profoundly influenced by past learning experiences. This is not, of course, to deny the reality of the emotional drive which motivates the behaviour, but simply to emphasize that the *manner* in which it is expressed is socially conditioned.

Learning of this kind begins in earliest infancy, with what is surely one of the first discoveries—namely that smiling by the baby is likely to lead to a warm response, perhaps a kiss or a cuddle, or at least increased eye contact, from mother or father. With the passing months, scores of tiny pieces of behaviour like this are learned and come together to make a pattern which may help or hinder relations with other people in the future. It seems clear, of course, that the way individual children take advantage of a given set of learning experiences will vary widely in accordance with their own predispositions; the introversion–extraversion scale developed by Eysenck is an illustration of the continuum which exists, apparently as an inherited factor, between individuals. Such an observation certainly accords with the experience of many parents who, discerning a difference in personality between two children from the earliest days, see them develop into a rather quiet, withdrawn elder and a sociable, outgoing younger (or vice versa) despite their encountering the same opportunities for learning. At whatever age and in whatever circumstances, the use we make of learning experiences will remain a matter for personal choice.

It is possible, however, to identify specific factors in the environment which may foster the development of social skills and particularly important among these is the presence of suitable models from whom the child may learn by example. The child who has active, sociable parents who greet neighbours in a friendly, outgoing way and frequently invite them into the house has a marked advantage in social learning in comparison with another who has no father and a mother who is too depressed and withdrawn to make the effort towards any social contacts and does not even respond much to the child. The opportunity for children to meet numbers of other children and adults, in their own home, the homes of others and in playgroups, provides very valuable opportunities to develop skills in the years before schooling begins, and early experiences in school can themselves be particularly crucial. Children whose attempts at communication are received with warmth and approval will be encouraged to repeat and develop them. It has become a truism to say that when children are enabled to feel happy and secure, then they will also be able to learn readily and to experiment and explore; but it can also be helpful to pinpoint those details which help them to feel secure in their exploration and learning—encouragement, approval and reinforcement.

Conversely, other factors may have an adverse effect on learning. Any form of social isolation may do so, whether it arises from living in a flat in a tower block or in a cottage at the end of a long farm track, or from a limitation on contacts with others outside the immediate family circle. Meeting with a hostile, rejecting response can be expected to have an inhibiting effect, as might happen in the case of a black child repeatedly rejected by the white youngsters in the neighbourhood; the same might apply to any child who was conspicuously different from his peers—possessing a hare lip or physical disability, or simply being fatter, or poorer, than the others. Any such overt difference may provoke a hostile response to the youngster, whose developing social skills may atrophy in consequence. Another less obvious adverse factor is a pattern of responses —usually from adults in this case—characterized by criticism and disapproval. A child whose efforts at social intercourse are frequently met with disapproval and negative comments and who is consistently blamed for failing to get things quite right is likely to become inhibited and show a tendency to withdraw from social interaction, or possibly to compensate and try to protect himself by developing an overassertive, almost aggressive style of presenting himself to disguise this underlying lack of confidence and fear of further disapproval.

While it can be useful to recognize that such factors in past history may have contributed to the development of current social behaviour, an understanding of this process is unlikely in itself to enable us to change this behaviour; new learning experiences are needed to provide an opportunity for the development of new patterns. Such new experiences do often occur unplanned, perhaps as a by-product of some other change like leaving home and going to college, or almost accidentally, as when a new family moves in next door and new friendships are made in consequence; sometimes they are sought deliberately, but quite naturally, in the ordinary run of things, as when an adolescent or young adult joins a youth club. This last might be particularly important for a youngster who found it quite easy to make friends in the fairly structured setting of his school, but lacks the skills needed to get to know new people once he has left school, when he may be much less clear what is expected of him.

People who want to develop their communication skills in a particular direction, such as teachers and social workers in training, or possibly those who wish to become active in politics, may also find it desirable to seek out some special environment in which they can test out and develop the skills which their new activities will require. The second section of this book is concerned with this process of testing out and development as we have experienced it with groups of social workers in training. The third section, describing social skills groups in both field and residential settings, is concerned with the provision of new learning experiences for people who, for one reason or another, have not developed ways of interacting with other people which satisfy them, and who feel generally uncomfortable and insecure in social situations where most of us would find this unwarranted. The work described in both these sections rests on the central assumption that it is often helpful to experiment and learn, and to experience the challenge of "difficult" situations, in a simulation in the relatively safe environment of a supportive group before making the attempt in actuality.

It may be helpful to consider at this point some general factors which may influence and possibly interfere with new learning experiences. For many people, an essential first stage is actually to *un*learn some existing bits of behaviour. One person may persistently look at the ground when talking, or cover her mouth with a hand; another may "pick" at himself continuously or scratch his head or his beard, all without realizing it. All these behaviours have the effect of diminishing markedly the quality of the individual's inter-action with others, and yet they are often quite persistent, so that it requires a high degree of perseverance to eliminate or reduce them. Yet it may be very important to do so, particularly for someone entering the helping professions: if a counsellor or social worker has a number of very irritating mannerisms, many clients may find this so distracting that it becomes impossible for them to communicate in a relaxed way and to confide as they may need to do. A similar pattern of behaviour might detract from the ability to convey a professional level of competence in formal group settings, such as a case conference or magistrates' court. A real effort may thus have to be made to unlearn any item of behaviour which has this kind of effect.

Certain kinds—indeed most kinds—of handicap also present par-ticular difficulties in social skills learning. In particular, blind people are inevitably deprived of the visual cues on which the rest of us rely heavily in our interaction with others; this also makes it specially difficult for them to give out the "right" kind of non-verbal cues when talking to sighted people. Thus blind children may have to be taught specifically to stand facing the other person, and even how to smile, since looking and smiling at an acquaintance are generally accepted signals that we want to open a conversation. There are necessarily special difficulties in the context of mental handicap about explaining the purpose and establishing goals for social skills training. In the third section of this book some illustrations will be given of such difficulties and how they may be approached, on the basis of actual programmes worked out with staff from group care settings.

A final factor which may hamper the learning of new behaviour lies in the consequences of individuals being given some stigmatizing label, often of a psychiatric kind. Thus others in their environment may continue to respond to them in terms of their label and the expectations it arouses, thrusting them back into a morass of passiv-ity and inertia. There is a chilling example of this cited by Rosenhan (1973): a bogus patient addressed a quite ordinary question to one of the doctors on the ward and was totally ignored—presumably because his question was viewed not as a piece of social interaction requiring a response, but merely as a behavioural symptom of someone who was just a "case", not a person. People who have spent a lot of time in institutions such as psychiatric hospitals also display various kinds of "odd" behaviour which almost invite rejection, and they may revert to such behaviour even when making progress in developing new ways of interacting if people in their environment respond to them just in terms of their identity as a member of some stigmatized or deviant group.

It is possible to distinguish a number of somewhat different approaches to social skills training (for instance those of Argyle, Priestley, or Liberman); moreover, in various fields of practice, including prisons and social work agencies, groups may be set up and run under a "social skills" title which cannot in fact be said to provide social skills training since no specific method is being followed. This chapter will conclude with a discussion of the essential elements of any programme of skills training, whether it be for the professional development of social workers and other helpers or for those receiving their help.

The first essential is the individual's motivation to change: in other words, the recognition of a difficulty, or some kind of gap, or some way of presenting her or himself that leads to problems with others, plus the belief that something can be done to improve this and that she or he will benefit from such a change. As suggested in the first chapter, a lot of work may have to be done with some clients, and indeed with some students and trainees, before this point of recognition, acknowledgement and hope is reached.

A second essential characteristic is that the work done is directed from the outset at identifying the actual situations in which the problem occurs or the deficit creates the difficulties in question; it has, moreover, to be specified in terms that the subject can do something about. Thus the general statement that "nobody ever talks to me" has to be refined into a single identifiable situation in which no conversation takes place, so that the subject can experiment with a different way, perhaps several ways, of behaving in this situation which may lead to a more satisfactory outcome.

A third feature which may be more or less explicit is the breaking down of quite complex patterns of behaviour into tiny discrete elements so that the one part that needs changing can be identified or so that, where a completely new pattern is being learned, one bit can be learned at a time. A vivid example of this latter kind of procedure could be seen when a residential worker with a group of mentally handicapped adults taught them to greet the local civic dignitaries when they came to visit, pinpointing all the elements of distance at which to stand, how to shake hands, how to smile, what to say. These new kinds of behaviour are rehearsed, not simply described, in the "safe" setting of the group (or simple one-to-one with the helper)—a fourth essential feature of the method, and perhaps the most characteristic of all. For many people, *repeated* rehearsal is needed, especially if the new behaviour is very different from the old or if the subject feels particularly anxious about it. It is crucial that this role-playing should be structured so that the performance can *succeed*, in the sense that an advance be made, no matter how tiny, from the previous one. Thus the individual can by small degrees come closer and closer to the point it is desired to reach, or the situations chosen will follow a progressive sequence from the easiest to the most difficult. The accent must always be on success rather than failure, so great care has to be taken not to allow role-plays to go on for too long, beyond the point at which the improvement made can be sustained.

Fifth and equally crucial is the practice of reinforcement: that is, always and immediately "rewarding" the central figure or figures in the role-play, selecting for special approval those things which they did well, or at the very least acknowledging and praising their courage in tackling something they clearly find very difficult. It can often tax the ingenuity of a worker to find something worthy of approval, but the effort has to be made and it can prove very worthwhile indeed since this could well be the first experience of social approval this particular subject has had. At the same time, in a group, the leaders have to encourage other members to add their own praise and support since they may need to learn how to be sympathetic, helpful and supportive to others at the same time as one of them is engaged on another piece of learning. This too is not an easy task: many group members are unused to receiving praise and approval, and this is related to the fact that they are also unused to giving it. Example is not always enough: it sometimes needs to be made quite explicit that destructively critical comments are unhelpful and therefore to be avoided, that people need and benefit from encouragement and that any comments added afterwards need to be in the positive direction of suggesting something that it would be helpful to do differently. The standing temptation to jump in straight away with a critical comment "Oh no, you did that quite wrong", is a most powerful one and none of us, whether social worker, group member or leader, can afford to believe ourselves exempt from it. We all need a constant reminder (albeit self-administered) to reinforce, encourage, support.

A sixth factor, which can have a very significant influence on progress, is "homework": the practice outside the actual learning sessions of the skills, or elements of skills, that are being learned. A task to be carried out by each group member between weekly sessions on which she or he can report in the ensuing one is a very valuable element in the learning, though the special problems presented by total institutions such as prisons must be evident. In other settings, however, it is often helpful to encourage pairings between group members to carry out assignments involving visiting places like bars, clubs or shops.

This device of selecting homework assignments between working sessions may be seen as part of, or closely related to, the final element in the approach: that of generalization, the process by which what has been practised in simulation is acted out in the real-life situation and becomes part of the individual's total range of behaviour and capacities for interacting with others. Being able to do something in a role-play is no guarantee of performance in the world outside, especially in a situation of especial stress. Yet it is possible to cite examples of people who have done precisely that. In *Achieving Change in Social Work* (Collins and Collins 1981) we described how a young woman took the initiative in conversations with her neighbour, with the result that she no longer felt compelled to avoid him for fear he would talk about a subject which distressed her. An adolescent boy who returned home after a period at an intermediate treatment centre found himself in the middle of one of the violent rows that had characterized his recent relationship with his mother; he broke off and said to her, "I talked about this sort of thing at the centre and I realized that it never gets us anywhere. What we have to do is give ourselves time to cool down, then talk it over quietly". Discussing this with him afterwards, a social worker commented on how difficult it must have been to do and he explained that he had role-played it while at the centre.

Another aspect of generalization lies in the ability to transfer behaviour that has been learned in relation to one problem situation to others not the same but requiring a similar kind of response. It is much harder to gauge whether this has in fact been done, but it seems reasonable to hope that the residents at the hostel for mentally handicapped adults were more able to meet and greet people generally, not just the civic dignitaries, and that the adolescent boy would be more able to break off quarrels at an early stage whoever the other party might be. This kind of generalization can be encouraged by discussion in the group, and also by helping members to seek out new settings in which their new skills may be practised.

The first stage of any effective programme of skills training must be a realistic and reliable assessment. It is accordingly to this topic that we now turn.

CHAPTER 3   Assessment, feedback and evaluation

Assessment is a function of central importance in all forms of education and training: someone has to assess what the subject is able to do at the outset of the educational process, what are the particular areas in which that person experiences difficulties and what are the knowledge and skills that need to be developed. During the educational process, there needs to be continuous monitoring of what the subject is learning and feedback should be given regularly and frequently about the progress that is being made. Finally, there must be some final evaluation to assess the learning that has taken place.

In no form of learning is this assessment element more vital than in that of training in professional and social skills. In this it recalls our previous analogy with musical skills—imagine trying to learn to sing without getting feedback from others or by listening to a recording of one's performance! What the singer hears always differs from what others hear because of the effects of bone conduction through the skull; it is equally true that the way we perceive ourselves in interaction with others often differs from their perception in quite significant ways, and we need to be made aware of this. To develop this awareness, we need very specific information: not that we often antagonize people or make it easy for them to ignore us, but that when we did or said a particular thing on a certain occasion it had the effect in question.

All of this applies with equal force to social skills work with clients and to the development of professional skills, and this fact, together with the central importance of the topic, means that it is appropriate at this point to proceed to a detailed discussion of assessment, with some practical suggestions of methods which may be found helpful. Hence this chapter falls broadly into three sections, the first being concerned with assessment in terms equally applicable to professional and to social skills training, the second with the assessment of workers' professional skills, and the third with assessing clients' social skills.

The very term "assessment" is itself used in a variety of ways in the social work literature. In work with clients it is generally employe· to refer to the initial stages of involvement, and indeed in some case such assessment can constitute the whole of the involvemenι. Where students are concerned, the term is more frequently used to describe the evaluation which takes place at the end of a stage of learning and here it usually includes some judgement on the adequacy of the performance—a pass/fail decision. Assessment of some kind also continues throughout the process of professional training, with an element of feedback to the student from those responsible for the training, and throughout the helping process, with feedback to client from worker. What follows here is intended to be applicable to assessment at whatever stage it takes place, unless this is indicated by the use of the terms "initial" or "evaluation".

BESTRIDE: A GENERAL ASSESSMENT SCHEME

While it is clearly behaviour that is the most conspicuous object of assessment, so that it is logical to take it as the first subject for consideration here, it must nevertheless not be overlooked that it represents only one element. In order to ensure that all the relevant factors in the assessment are borne in mind, it is useful to devise some sort of mnemonic. The one we are suggesting here uses the word BESTRIDE to indicate the eight relevant elements; this is in fact a revised formulation of one we have previously put forward (Collins and Collins 1981) which was derived from the BASIC ID multimodal analysis of Lazarus (1976). The present formulation uses the more familiar terms "emotion" and "thinking" rather than "affect" and "cognition", and it adds a further consideration, that of the environment, to complete the picture. Such a scheme can offer a useful method of analysing an individual's competence in interaction into the following elements:

- Behaviour
- Emotions
- Sensation
- Thinking

- Relationships
- Imagery
- Drugs
- Environment

The initial letters of these categories make up the mnemonic BESTRIDE.

Behaviour

This is the obvious starting point in the assessment of social skills, as indeed in all assessment. Does the subject talk too little or too much? Is she or he passive or overassertive? And who is to decide, when once we have a clear impression of how the person is behaving, whether that behaviour is deficient, excessive or about right? There is no infallible answer to questions like these, and the only general statement it seems safe to make is that extremes ought to be avoided: that people who either talk ceaselessly or never say a word are seldom perceived as acting acceptably. Where professionals are concerned, it can be useful to take account of the preferences expressed by clients, who are more likely to complain that workers say too little or are too passive in interviews (Mayer and Timms 1970; Sainsbury 1975; Rees and Wallace 1982). Clients are more likely to be referred for social skills training if they are tongue-tied and inhibited than if they are compulsive talkers, though both kinds of problem may be encountered.

Behaviour can usefully be broken down into discrete elements such as eye contact, proximity and posture; non-verbal behaviour can be just as important as speech. Posture and facial expression are particularly crucial, and can totally negate the message being conveyed verbally if they are inappropriate to it, since people frequently attach more significance or credence to the non-verbal messages they receive than to the actual words spoken. Speech, too, needs to be broken down into components—not only the words used, but volume, speed and pitch, together with fluency or hesitancy.

Any assessment of interpersonal behaviour needs to take account of its context: when and where is it displayed, and with whom? Many people experience difficulties in specific contexts only, while other situations present no problems for them, so precision about the other actors and the background can be just as important as precision about the performance.

Emotions

The person for whom all social encounters give rise only to positive emotions such as pleasure, enjoyment and satisfaction is fortunate indeed—and, it may be suspected, rare. Negative emotions such as fear, anxiety and embarrassment can interfere with many a social performance, with consequent anger, frustration, shame and disappointment. The latter group of feelings experienced after interchange with others are often a signal to us that we have not played our part in them to our own satisfaction, but they are certainly not an infallible guide to the adequacy of our performance. People whose self-awareness is limited may very readily feel satisfied with a performance of very low standard, and while this might not matter with a client for whom the aim was primarily to increase satisfaction with social contacts, in the case of a professional from whom a specified standard of performance is required those feelings of satisfaction might require some challenge. On the other hand, the self-critical individual, whether worker or client, very readily feels disappointed and dissatisfied with her or his own achievements because they fall short of perfection. Again, the feeling needs to be pinpointed, and perhaps challenged.

Where negative emotions are experienced before performance, they need to be recognized and identified but not lingered over. To say, as is often said by helpers of many different theoretical persuasions, that one "must stick with the anxiety" does not mean wallowing in the awfulness and destructiveness of the emotion but staying with the anxiety-provoking situation and working on it. It is useful to remember, too, that although clients and workers may find themselves in different kinds of situations, and with different demands being made on them, the actual emotions experienced in these difficult situations are often the same—something which can be a great help in empathizing with clients. It can sometimes be helpful to share such feelings with clients, for whom it can be a source of reassurance to know that for professionals too there are situations that cause great anxiety and that lead to our being just as dissatisfied with ourselves as they are with themselves.

Sensation

The sensations associated with social anxiety are well known because they are so widely experienced; almost everyone must be familiar with symptoms such as nausea, "butterflies in the stomach", palpitations, dryness in the mouth and others more personal to the individual. Techniques of anxiety management developed in recent years involve recognizing these sensations for what they are, understanding something of the mechanisms which provoke them in any individual conscious of external threat, and developing strategies for reducing their strength and their potential for incapacitating us—relaxation exercises, for instance. Most courses of skills training can usefully include some teaching about such techniques for coping with anxiety in social situations. Professionals, it is true, are unlikely to have the opportunity to practise full-scale relaxation just before a stressful interview or other encounter, but it can still be valuable to learn to identify some actions such as taking a few deep breaths or adopting a more relaxed and comfortable posture which will alleviate the feelings of discomfort.

Thinking

The importance of thought processes is now increasingly recognized in skills training generally, especially the kind of "self-talk" or "internal dialogue" characterized by negative thoughts which either predict calamity—such as "This'll be a disaster" or "I can't cope with this"—or express destructive self-criticism such as "That was terrible—I made a complete mess of it". Negative thinking can take some characteristic forms which are especially undermining for professionals: they include the nagging doubt that "I don't have any real right to be here" and the self-questioning "Who am I to tell other people how to lead their lives?" or "Why should these people listen to my opinion anyway?" Self-doubt of this kind can be fostered by media criticisms of social work and perhaps too by some critical academic input on training courses, so that workers in training often need to spend some time in establishing clearly in their own minds what is the professional base from which they are operating. A well-thought-out professional position which takes full account both of ethical considerations and of the limitations to what is realistically achievable is an essential prerequisite for skilful practice and can lead to much more constructive patterns of thinking about the challenges which the worker is about to face, for instance: "I have the responsibility to ensure the safety of this child, if necessary in spite of the parents' opposition", "It is my job to offer help to families who are in some difficulty" or "I have considered the situation carefully and this is my professional opinion".

There are more common forms of negative thinking which have been identified as having an inhibiting effect on people in general, and they can usually be recognized by the presence of one or more of the following characteristics:

1. They predict the future, for example "I'll make a mess of it".
2. They assert as fact something for which there is no evidence, for example "People are always criticizing me behind my back".
3. They are expressed in extreme terms, for example "That was a disaster! I'm a complete failure".
4. They are unhelpful and disabling, for example "I'm no good at this".

Once the ability to identify such thoughts has developed it is possible to go on to substitute more positive thoughts such as "That wasn't marvellous, but it wasn't the end of the world either, and if I practise I'll be able to do it even better next time".

Clients can be helped to identify some more specific thoughts too, such as "I'm a complete failure as a mother because my child has been taken into care"; quite a lot of work would have to be done here before such a mother might be able to say to herself instead: "I've had my problems and that's why my baby was taken away, but that doesn't mean I'm a completely bad person and if I go on working on the problems I'll be able to look after her all right". But some such change in the mother's thinking will be needed if she is to become able to interact with her child in a relaxed and satisfying way.

It is particularly hard to establish what thoughts mentally handicapped people may have about themselves and their capacities. A group of workers in this field, following a course option on social skills training and discussing this subject with us, came to the conclusion that thoughts such as "I'm dependent" and "I need help" were characteristic of many of their clients. Such thoughts, which are often fostered by the over-protective behaviour of others around them, are not particularly helpful to them, and could usefully be given a more positive turn to become "With a bit of help I'll be able to do this" and "I can learn how to manage for myself".

Relationships

Like other elements in this analysis, existing relationships can either facilitate or inhibit social performance. Parents of handicapped youngsters may encourage them to remain within the "safe" confines of family relationships and actively discourage external contacts. A social services team too may have the same kind of effect (albeit more subtly) on its members if, by generating a cosy atmosphere and constantly looking inwards, it discourages members from developing contacts and cooperation with other agencies and exploiting community resources.

These relationships may, of course, also furnish the raw material of the work to be done, or at least an example of it: for instance, we describe in Chapter 10 a piece of work done by a group of youngsters in a children's home on some aspects of their interaction with other residents. Relationships between family members can furnish similar examples: conflicts between parents and adolescent children, for instance, or a mother's difficulties in interacting with her baby. For the professional, relationships within a team, especially an interdisciplinary one, may be relevant and may similarly offer material to work on, especially if there is an unequal distribution of power and status within the team.

Imagery

There are two kinds of mental image in particular which can affect and undermine social performance: first, the image of oneself as an incompetent, bungling idiot, and secondly, that of the perfect performer, whose characteristics will naturally vary according to context but who will always display the perfect combination of qualities which the situation demands—a Casanova chatting to women or a Perry Mason arguing his case in court. Many workers are particularly vulnerable to the influence of such images of the ideal performance, and young students often describe themselves as being undermined and constrained, prevented from responding naturally, by some notion of an "ideal worker" to which they ought to approximate. Images of this kind can lead to the striking of all kinds of forced and unconvincing postures: "I'm just like you really", which can emerge in reaction to what is perceived as false professionalism, carries no conviction whatever with clients, who know quite well that professional helpers are *not* just like themselves. Other images which a worker may project include "champion of the oppressed", "guru", "therapist" or "expert", and while these may not be harmful in themselves, they may fail to connect with what the client actually needs. One of the authors recalls attending a case review with, among others, the client concerned, and observing a counsellor sitting—almost lying—back in an easy chair with one leg thrown over the other, a "laid-back" attitude which did not commend itself to the client whose life was under discussion and which can surely only be understood in terms of the image he was trying to project.

Special importance must be attached to the images which handicapped people have both of themselves and of others. Handicap, physical handicap especially, can profoundly damage the image which the handicapped person has of the self in comparison with others. It is, moreover, especially difficult for people with sensory impairment to have a clear, accurate picture of the outside world, yet for them above all people it is particularly important to have reliable factual information about new situations they will be entering. A worker attending a strange court needs a clear picture of who will be where and what the usual procedures are; a blind person will need much more minute and detailed information about even very simple settings, such as where and how many the steps are, where to locate seats and obstacles, and so on. In default of such precise information, the world is a very dangerous and frightening place for handicapped people.

Drugs—and general physiological state

A wide range of drugs are commonly taken to alleviate anxiety and promote a feeling of well-being; they include prescribed drugs such as antidepressants and tranquillizers which, in large doses, may lead to a general damping down of responses and a "flat" presentation of the self. It is among the aims of skills training to diminish the need for such medication by teaching people to handle their social anxieties. Similar considerations apply to socially sanctioned drugs such as alcohol and tobacco, and it can be important to be aware of the special difficulties experienced by someone trying to stop drinking or smoking; alcoholics, for instance, sometimes report that they feel too anxious to initiate any social contacts at all unless they have taken one or two drinks, while several drinks may lead to a level of inhibition which is unacceptably low in the sense that totally uninhibited behaviour can easily become intolerable to others.

Environment

The effect of relationships with others in the environment has already been discussed. With regard to changes in the individual's behaviour, however, there are additional questions to be asked. Will the environment oppose or reverse any changes? Or will it foster or maintain them? Chapter 11 describes how a worker with deaf adolescents, mindful of this consideration, had to circulate a message among his colleagues: "Andy is learning how to greet people appropriately—please be sure to give approval when he does so". Sometimes it is necessary actually to create a new environment in which the skills learned can be practised, such as an alcohol-free bar where drinkers and non-drinkers can socialize without pressure on those trying to give up drinking.

Since the approach of this book is that there is no essential distinction between the skills required of professional workers and any other social skills, the above assessment categories are equally relevant to workers and clients. Some aspects of assessment are, however, more relevant to professional workers, and to these we now turn.

ASSESSING WORKERS' INTERPERSONAL SKILLS

The two principal approaches which may be taken to the assessment of workers' social skills could be described as the systematic and the problem-focused approaches. The systematic approach uses an inventory of the social skills to be expected of a professional worker at a particular stage of development while the problem-focused approach invites workers to identify, possibly with tutorial help, situations which they experience as especially stressful and difficult or in which their performance seems to indicate problems. Each method has its own strengths and weaknesses.

The systematic approach requires an inventory or checklist of the skills used in interaction; the list needs to be clear, detailed, coherent and exhaustive. A worker's ability to use each individual skill appropriately and effectively can then be assessed in terms of the level of attainment to be expected at the stage of development in question, levels which will necessarily vary with expectations of the worker based on previous training and experience.

There are disadvantages to this approach, exhaustive though it is, in that it does not necessarily highlight the areas in which difficulty is experienced. A worker's social skills in understanding and responding to a client may be assessed as satisfactory in a relatively straightforward and non-taxing situation, but the same worker might well display a far lower level of confidence and competence with particularly difficult, intransigent individuals or in situations with a threatening or daunting component. Hostile or aggrieved clients, situations where the welfare of children is at issue and participation in court work all make demands on workers' skills in interaction. The inherent difficulties of these situations are often intensified by aggressive, domineering or manipulative behaviour on the part of other actors in the scene: performance in court, for instance, may be undermined by hostile or belligerent defence counsel seeking to discredit the worker's evidence. Critical or insensitive behaviour by court staff may also be experienced as very threatening.

Appropriate training can help enormously in building up a good level of competence in these very difficult situations, and the best way for this competence to be assessed is for the workers concerned to identify themselves those situations and individuals with which they find it hardest to deal. It is often the function or status itself of other actors in the situation, like lawyers, judges or hospital consultants, that causes or intensifies the problem. A sense of awe towards such figures is largely engendered by doubts about our own professional status and competence, associated with a poor image of ourselves as professional people, and self-assessment can help to highlight influential cognitive factors like this.

Any written series of objectives for practice has inevitable pitfalls in its use. Because professional helping, whatever the context, is essentially a dynamic, evolving process, any evaluation of it which is to have validity must not be artificial or rigid; hence the system of assessment which we are putting forward here needs to be used very flexibly. Such assessment instruments are essentially guidelines, around which a creative and sensitive appreciation of all the worker's skills may coalesce into a tangible and usable form. The system specifies clearly the activity being assessed (observing, giving feedback, etc), with the level of performance expected varying according to the practice situation and the degree of sophistication of the student or worker. There must, moreover, be an explicit understanding between the subject of the assessment and those carrying it out about the level of skill expected and about the kind of evidence which will be regarded as satisfactory proof of ability to display the skills in question. Table 3.1 gives a specimen assessment schedule adapted from that used on an in-service course for evaluating students at various stages in their professional training. It will be noted that for each individual skills objective there is a corresponding positive or negative indicator which functions as criterion of the presence of the skill in question.

Obtaining Material as a Basis for Evaluation

Theoretically, there are a variety of ways in which material could be obtained for evaluating a worker's practice skills, but some methods with quite a valuable potential are little used in practice. We might, for instance, ask clients how they would rate a worker's skills, but this would be a time-consuming, delicate undertaking and moreover raises problems of confidentiality. Considerations of confidentiality may similarly preclude direct observation, but it would be most unfortunate if such considerations were to exclude any part the client's response to the worker might have to play in the evaluation. Consumer studies generally have a most important contribution to make to the maintenance of a high standard of practice.

Table 3.1.   Worker skills assessment scheme

Interpersonal skills	Assessment indicator	
	Positive	Negative
Basic level		
1. Observation		
Demonstrate observation skills to the extent that she/he can:		
(a) Describe accurately and fully the physical characteristics of a person	(a) A systematic and comprehensive description	(a) Uses vague, generalized descriptions; overpreoccupation with one characteristic
(b) Describe what the person was doing over a specific time, noting behaviour, verbal/non-verbal activity	(b) Detailed description of specific verbal and non-verbal behaviour	(b) Only notices verbal activity; only notices non-verbal activity; premature interpretation of behaviour; notices and recalls very little; only generalized impression
(c) Specify two episodes of interaction (i) one-to-one, (ii) small groups, and describe own behaviour and the interaction within each	(c) Systematic approach to observing and reporting observations; takes account of everyone's behaviour including passive members	(c) Cannot distinguish between process and content; cannot describe own behaviour; cannot see causes and effects of behaviour; overpreoccupation with most conspicuous behaviour
2. Listening		
Demonstrate listening skills to the extent that she/he can convey back to another person the substance of what the person has said to their satisfaction, during a specified interaction	Clear repetition of message	Message distorted by own thoughts and feelings; tries to remember too much

3. *Questioning*		
(a) Use open and closed questions selectively in order to gain information	Demonstrates ability to distinguish open and closed questions and use appropriately; prompts selectively	Cannot satisfactorily distinguish or use selectively
(b) Use open and closed questions and prompting techniques selectively in order to enable the expression of ideas and feelings	Demonstrates ability to distinguish open and closed questions and use appropriately; prompts selectively	Cannot satisfactorily distinguish or use selectively
4. *Information-giving*		
Can give appropriate information clearly and efficiently	Information appropriate to situation. Client's response indicates understanding	Too much/too little detail; assumes knowledge client does not have; no check client has understood
5. *Group participation*		
Actively contribute to the maintenance/development of a group and to the attainment of its agreed task(s) and describe two skills she/he has used in the process	Responds positively to the ideas, feelings of others. Can identify a range of helpful and unhelpful behaviours	Ignores, neglects tasks; ignores, neglects feelings, needs of others; dominated by own needs, ideas; easily diverted, distracts members
Second level		
1. Demonstrate listening skills to the extent that she/he can accurately feed back feeling as well as content and pick up "clues"	Can feed back feeling and pick up clues	Does not pick up feelings and feed back
2. Convey respect and warmth	Can convey concern and interest by flexible response	Uses stereotyped responses; preoccupied with task or self; predetermines client's needs/views

(Continued)

Table 3.1. (*Continued*)

Interpersonal skills	Assessment indicator	
	Positive	Negative
3. Demonstrate empathy	Client seems satisfied that her/his feelings are understood and work moves on	Clients make repeated efforts to express feelings or "switch off"
4. Use special verbal and non-verbal techniques to communicate with clients with a limited or impaired capacity for communication	Gives attention to selection and use of vocabulary, tone and pitch and pace of voice, complexity of message and environment	Does not pay adequate attention to client's needs or environmental demands/constraints
5. Identify the implications of what is expressed in terms of patterns and recurring themes	Can summarize main implications of process and content of the interviews; direct focus of interview to significant areas	Selects at random parts of interview for attention. Preoccupied with own priorities and ideas
6. Structure discussions/interviews in terms of beginning, developing, ending, working at the client's (other person's) pace	Begins to phase and structure selectively	Remains haphazard; unaware of need, structure and pace
7. Observe the behaviour of individual clients and groups in interaction with significant others—peers, families, communities, to the extent that this can be accurately described	Accurate description of observed behaviour	Cannot distinguish between process and content; cannot describe own behaviour; cannot see causes and effects of behaviour; overpreoccupation with most conspicuous behaviour

8. Initiate and lead a group in the work setting enabling the attainment of its agreed task and describe two leadership skills used in the process	Prepares self and others for the group activity; prepares physical environment; enables participation; is aware of emotional climate; enables group to develop; performs leadership tasks appropriate to group's purpose (eg discussion group, task group, recreation, etc)	Motivation of members not sustained, dominates or overdirects group so that members become passive, leave, rebel, become anxious; group confusion caused by lack of information or direction
9. Maintain open communication (avoid blocking) with clients who experience stress, anxiety, loss, change	Shows sensitive, flexible response in crisis situations	Cannot respond appropriately
10. Give positive reinforcement to enable the development of self-confidence, self-esteem	Acknowledges strength and progress	Patronizes clients; uses false reassurance; gives unconstructive criticism
11. Demonstrate sensitivity in the performance of intimate physical tasks for clients	Encourages independence wherever possible; meets privacy needs; asks client how she/he wants things	Is hurried with completion of task; talks to colleagues over client's head
12. Give advice appropriately and clearly	Outlines options available; sets out possible course(s) of action and consequences	Retreats when asked for advice; intrudes advice; fails to clarify steps needed/consequences

The use of audio and video recording to monitor practice is becoming increasingly widespread and can be very useful, but this also (video particularly) can be seen as presenting problems of confidentiality and the presence of recording equipment in the interview room can be inhibiting. There are, however, some forms of practice, such as family therapy, in which the use of equipment is well established and accepted both by practitioners and by clients, and the same applies to much social skills training with clients—it is accepted as "part of the package"—and problem-focused work with students.

Written records have hitherto been the most frequently used material for assessment; process recordings in particular can be a valuable tool for both learner and teacher, and compiling and analysing a process recording provides an opportunity to reflect at length about the various aspects of a piece of interaction. The problem in evaluation, however, arises from the worker's investment in what she or he is describing, which imbues that description with a high degree of subjectivity. While such bias may be challenged by the assessors, it is doubtful whether they can always penetrate behind what is being presented.

Examples

Nick submitted some work for assessment which included a video recording showing some unhelpful and inappropriate pieces of non-verbal behaviour by himself which created an impression very different from that of the process recording. It was not that there had been deliberate omissions or misrepresentation in the record; Nick had simply not been aware of what he was communicating non-verbally.

Similarly, Timms (1972, Appendix) gives three recordings of the same interview, brief, process and verbatim. Significantly, only the verbatim account (transcribed from tape) provides evidence that the client is not entirely satisfied with the service she has received. The negatives she expresses are not recorded, probably because they were never picked up by the social worker.

The presence of a participant observer in the assessed work is a device which has been relatively neglected in the past, apart from group care settings, in which it can be introduced quite naturally because teams of workers are already operating together. Nothing is quite as effective as working together with a group of clients in enabling the assessor to get the "feel" of the worker's approach. Individual style is difficult to assess at a distance, whereas joint working offers a unique opportunity to pick up the worker's strengths and weaknesses. Often, of course, this kind of participation is not possible and here the use of role-plays and simulation offers a valuable compromise between actually seeing the worker in action with clients and accepting a second-hand account of the work.

Assessment during in-service training has one further component: the contribution of the student's line manager (immediately responsible superior). This contribution is essentially advisory, since the manager must be aware of the work being undertaken but often does not participate in it. The student may not have to show a detailed record of the work undertaken for assessment to the manager but the manager's comments on the student's performance should be obtained by anyone responsible for assessing the student's learning. The weight to be attached to such comments necessarily varies according to the work situation, and the complexity of relationships and interactions within the agency can militate against the neutrality of the line manager, who is quite correctly seen as contributing to the process but not responsible for it.

Using Simulations as Forum for Assessing Problems of Performance

We have stressed the value of simulation and role-play as a compromise solution where practice cannot be observed *in vivo*; such an approach also has, of course, the advantage that participants can improve and develop their skills and so need not be dejected about making a mess of things. Video recording of such simulations is (relatively) problem-free and offers the possibility of instant feedback to performers, even without the comments and suggestions of observers.

In our professional training practice, we find that students benefit from focusing both on varied, personally selected aspects of their own skills and on developing the particular style of working (and combination of skills) required for helping clients to develop their own social skills. The selection of individual areas to work on can be aided by the use of a questionnaire such as the version we have used (Table 3.2) for several years to pinpoint the problems experienced by students. The list has, however, never been treated as exhaustive and students frequently bring examples from their practice experience. In sessions like these, assessment is largely self-assessment and people choose what they want to focus on; feedback is constant and immediate and the element of evaluation in the pass/fail sense is entirely absent. Of course, anyone conducting such a group cannot fail to make some kind of judgement about performances, but this needs to be expressed to the person concerned and only transmitted to others such as a tutor with her or his consent; anything more formal would imperil the commitment members are asked to make to venture into precisely those areas which they find most difficult and to take risks in order to make progress.

Evaluating the performance of students acting as social skills trainers themselves is quite a complex matter. They can and do, of course, receive feedback at frequent intervals when running simulated groups, just as they do in any other kind of role-play. But beyond this point a difference emerges between students following a college-based course and those on an in-service course. College students are largely dependent on the opportunities a placement can offer them and may not have the chance of applying their knowledge of social skills training methods in any given placement. On the other hand, workers receiving in-service training, already familiar with their clients and work setting, can design an appropriate project and carry it out. This piece of practice can then be evaluated by means of a written account of it and also, in many instances, with the actual participation of a tutor in some of the work. Here we have a perfect example of that direct observation of the subject at work which gives the most vivid and reliable impression of that person's capacities. The whole process, indeed, offers a good general model for a piece of assessed learning: students can begin with a short block period of teaching on the theoretical basis for the approach, followed by an interval (perhaps three weeks) in which they set up their pieces of work, with some tutorial help. During a second block consisting of workshop sessions, difficulties can be discussed and ironed out, often in role-plays. Students then carry out their programmes and write them up for assessment

Table 3.2. Stressful situations questionnaire

Imagine yourself in each of the following situations; then try to
evaluate how anxious each one would make you feel and circle the
figure in the appropriate column

	Not particularly anxious	Slightly anxious	Fairly anxious	Very anxious
1. Presenting report in court—especially facing hostile questioning	0	1	2	3
2. Approaching member of another profession with high prestige (eg strange GP) with delicate request	0	1	2	3
3. Speaking before a large audience—eg introducing speaker to a meeting	0	1	2	3
4. Presenting a sustained argument to a large group of people and dealing with interruptions	0	1	2	3
5. Keeping control of an interview with an aggressive or dominating client	0	1	2	3
6. Sustaining your own point of view in a multidisciplinary setting, such as a hospital	0	1	2	3
7. Meeting the challenge (from a client) that you are too young/ inexperienced to be a help	0	1	2	3
8. Responding to racist or sexist remarks by clients or colleagues	0	1	2	3
9. Defending your handling of a situation which has turned out badly	0	1	2	3

(*Continued*)

Table 3.2. (*Continued*)

	Not particularly anxious	Slightly anxious	Fairly anxious	Very anxious
10. Explaining your identity and mission in a delicate situation, eg to a mother who has been anonymously accused of ill-treating children	0	1	2	3
11. Defending your department, or social workers in general, against criticisms you feel are partly justified	0	1	2	3
12. Making an apology for a serious error, and pitching it right	0	1	2	3

according to clear-cut criteria of their ability to understand and apply the theory and use it to help their clients. Participation by the tutor and study supervisor in the work done not only contributes to the accuracy of the evaluation but also can provide the student with continuous feedback during the time the task is being carried out. It is programmes which have been set up and monitored in this way which form the material for most of the case studies in Section III.

METHODS OF ASSESSING CLIENTS FOR SOCIAL SKILLS TRAINING

Social skills assessment can involve a variety of methods and instruments, the choice depending largely on the client group involved but to some extent also on the preferences and the imagination of the worker. Many residential institutions already have established procedures for assessing new arrivals and these may have useful material to offer. However, it is notable in many institutions where the process of assessment is particularly thorough and wide-ranging that often very little use is made of many of the factors which emerge from it: short-stay children's homes often carry out full assessments of this kind, but no practical use is made of the findings to promote constructive change because of shortage of resources or lack of a method by which such change could be brought about. Some of the case studies in Section III incorporate elements of a general assessment carried out in the residential institution where the work was done before any question of skills training had arisen, since aspects of the social performance of handicapped children and young people were being assessed on admission and at intervals thereafter. In addition, the workers in these examples devised methods of their own, adapted to the needs and capacities of the clients they were working with. One of the most attractive features of the work described was the imaginative use of various assessment and monitoring devices, such as questionnaires, charts and graphs, designed not only to be comprehensible to the clients concerned but also to stimulate their interest and enthusiasm. It would be hard to imagine anything further removed from the arid statistical material which characterizes accounts of similar work in the professional journals of clinical psychology! The workers had clearly understood how important it is to involve clients fully from the outset in the assessment process, for they need to understand as fully as possible the reasons why the programme is being undertaken and the methods which will be used. Clearly this can be difficult, especially for clients with severe mental handicap, but it can be amazing how effective workers who are sensitive and empathetic and have a good knowledge of their client group can prove in enabling them to understand what is involved, commit themselves wholeheartedly to it and develop an awareness of progress made.

Irrespective of any more specialized approaches to the assessment, some kind of more general schedule such as the BESTRIDE system described above is likely to prove useful, if not essential, as most of the specialized instruments seem to lean very heavily towards the behavioural aspects, so that important elements such as self-image, thought processes and relationships with others in the environment may be left out of account.

So far as a general scheme for the assessment of behaviour is concerned, Table 3.3 provides a specimen which would be sufficiently comprehensive for most purposes although work with some

Table 3.3.   Social skills general assessment schedule

Components of social behaviour
Non-verbal responses: body posture, gestures and body movements, physical proximity, touch, eye contact, physical appearance, dress, etc, facial expression, smiling, head movements

Basic verbal responses: qualities of speech and voice, viz tone and pitch, volume, loudness, rate of chat, clarity of speech, latency of response (delay in answering), hesitations, lack of fluency

Content of speech
1. Relevance
2. Interruptions
3. Interest content
4. Repetitiveness

Listening skills
1. Acknowledgement
2. Reflection
3. Feedback responses
4. Personal self-discipline

Basic conversation skills
1. Initiating responses
2. Asking questions

Perception of emotion through
1. Facial expression
2. Posture
3. Voice quality
4. Gestures

Complex skills
A wide range of more sophisticated skills, eg acceptable group behaviour, work behaviour, leisure behaviour

Elements in the assessment of social skills
1. Direct observation
2. Questionnaires
3. Social skills chart
4. Construction of baseline of behaviour against which performance can be measured
5. Evaluation using specific behavioural objectives

client groups such as the handicapped might benefit from a few additions.

Choice of Focus

The material which it is proposed to work on may often be selected by the clients themselves. In Chapter 10, for instance, work is described with a group of boys in a children's home on temper tantrum control. It was particularly important in selecting this as the focus that it should be identified as a problem by the boys themselves, not imposed upon them because it was something which caused difficulties for the establishment. Moreover, the boys themselves chose another boy from the home to participate in the group as a model because they saw him as someone who was good at handling frustrating situations in an unaggressive way. This group provides a pleasing illustration of the general principle that clients should work on aspects of their performance which they themselves see as important and should be enabled to change their behaviour in directions of their own choosing. It may be necessary to enter something of a caveat here, in that it might occasionally happen that a client wished to develop a pattern of behaviour designed to exploit or manipulate other people. In theory, a would-be seducer might be seeking to develop a technique for making fast, superficial and exploitative relationships, or a member of a racist organization to whip up antagonism among his neighbours. The ethical duty to refuse to become involved in such objectives is as clear here as it would be with any other form of helping designed to enable clients to achieve their goals, but the general principle remains that the focus of work is decided in accordance with the client's wishes though there may need to be some preliminary negotiation before a decision is arrived at.

Sometimes the client may have a limited objective in mind which can, however, fall within a broader objective in that it will be useful in a variety of circumstances, not just in the context in which it was originally envisaged. The work with visually handicapped children described in Chapter 11 includes a child who wanted to learn how to telephone his parents, an objective which falls naturally within the wider area of telephone communication in general and which was a particularly suitable target to select since the child was strongly motivated to achieve it. In any case, the objective needs to be specified very precisely, since only so can the initial assessment baseline be drawn and progress towards the objective monitored. Thus the aim "to increase Mr Low's conversational ability" would be too general for these purposes and would require to be refor-mulated as the precise objective: "At the end of one month Mr Low will initiate and sustain two one-minute pieces of conversation with another group member". The maxims "Small is beautiful" and "Little and often" are a good guide to the practice of social skills training, which requires us to select small, discrete elements of behaviour and work them into a wider repertoire of performance. This whole process requires constant reassessment and feedback, together with periodic evaluation, but, precisely because it is so open, explicit and specific, the process also lends itself to constant assessment.

Baselines and the Measurement of Progress

Assessing social performance both initially and at appropriate intervals requires some kind of effective yardstick for measuring—or perhaps counting—successive performances. Some attempt must be made to measure the behaviour under scrutiny, or at least to gain some realistic and recordable definition of it in terms that will bear critical evaluation later. This "baseline" of behaviour (what is displayed at the outset) is easier to measure or count in relation to life skills such as dressing, toileting or other simple mechanical sequences of actions, where a number of concrete, readily identifiable and countable actions are concerned, but social skills involve subtleties of individual style, nuance and expression and are harder to pin down. Such difficulties increase as more complex situations are envisaged, calling for greater sophistication of response.

One of the most exciting developments in social skills training has been the increased use of video recording and most, though not all, of the work described in the case studies in Section III was carried out with the help of video equipment. Whereas workers and students often express intense anxiety about appearing on video, most clients love it: mentally handicapped people are especially enthusiastic. Here it can be possible to record a training programme in its entirety, from the first assessment right through to the final evaluation, thus providing feedback which is clear, simple and easily replicated. Very limited clients find little difficulty in recognizing what are the pieces of behaviour being referred to or in seeing the progress they are making. There are, however, a few clients with whom one would want to be very cautious about introducing the use of video: those who have a very idealized conception of their own performance or who suffer from extreme perfectionism, for instance, for whom the effect of seeing themselves on the screen at too early a stage might actually exacerbate their negative feelings about themselves. With such clients video must be introduced sensitively and gradually and the time chosen carefully; it sometimes helps if a vulnerable group member has an initial opportunity to view his or her performance in the company of just one worker rather than in front of the whole group.

If video is not available or not thought to be appropriate, an ordinary tape recorder can be used to good effect, and indeed has some advantages in that it is less conspicuous and potentially inhibiting and replay is even simpler. Successive performances can be readily compared to gauge the progress made and there is a permanent record available for use in later sessions if required. Some work on voice production using audio tapes with mentally handicapped young men is described in Chapter 12, and of course for the work with visually handicapped children this was the most appropriate medium. Both video and audio tape recording afford good opportunities for establishing reliable and durable records of clients' social performance to serve as a baseline and to monitor and evaluate progress. They are, however, not always available, and even when they are it is often desirable to support them with other methods.

Collecting Material for an Assessment

The range of materials available as evidence for the assessment of clients is similar to that discussed in relation to the evaluation of professional practice skills. Our initial knowledge of clients is likely to arise first from the experience of meeting them and secondly from the existence of records. Of course, the setting in which we first meet the client might be quite atypical and artificial, so that we might gain a misleading general impression from an early encounter. Records too may mislead, but equally they may offer a valuable guide to the worker by suggesting some tentative conclusions about the client's suitability for a particular programme, and indeed may also offer material for the assessment itself. Indications from the record concerning a client's health and welfare to date can be helpful, together with information about how she or he has coped and responded in the past. Records need to be used with caution, however, since there is often considerable speculation and opinion, perhaps even prejudice, mixed in with the factual information. While the opinions of responsible staff members should be given due consideration, it must be remembered that these opinions may be misinformed or may not hold good over time—what was true six months ago is not necessarily true now.

Again, as with the assessment of workers, it is useful to incorporate an element of self-report in addition to the opinions of others. "Others", moreover, can mean others in the client group rather than other members of staff, and where there is a conflict between pieces of material provided from these different sources it is impossible to make any automatic assumptions to the effect that one view is correct and the rest wrong. An interesting divergence of views is described in Chapter 12 in connection with some work with a group of profoundly deaf young men in an institution. The worker used a simple bipolar assessment (highly simplified version of Kelly grid) and was struck by the conflict of views about one of his clients between peers and staff members on characteristics like shy/not shy. Conflicts like this help to draw our attention to the situational factors which may make people present themselves now in one way, now in another. They also illustrate the significance of cultural variations (we often need to know what kind of behaviour is expected in a situation before we can judge whether the individual is performing adequately) and show how vital it is to have a thorough knowledge of the clients and setting in order to devise and apply the right sort of questionnaire or other assessment techniques.

Other methods of pencil-and-paper assessment which can be useful include checklists and a variety of charts. Generally it is best for workers to devise their own, but we offer two examples in Figures 3.1 and 3.2. Figure 3.1 is a target-type chart which has the advantage that it can show a range of factors but is essentially static, giving the position at one point in time, so a fresh chart is compiled to show the changed picture. The graph-type chart (Figure 3.2) can show day-to-day progression; this one is limited to a single factor but additional lines could be plotted to show others, especially to illustrate both the fading of problem behaviour and the development of positive features.

Always the participation of clients in the preparation and review of these assessments is most valuable; ensuring that clients can understand and participate means using care and imagination to devise the appropriate tools, and it is surprising how effectively this can be done even with severely handicapped clients. One worker devised a chart for use by her group of small children with severe learning

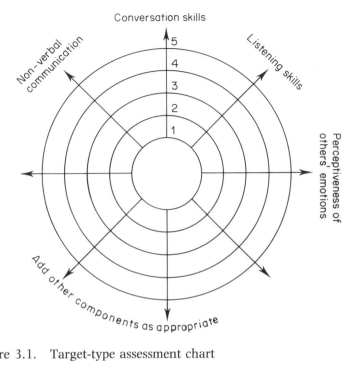

Figure 3.1. Target-type assessment chart

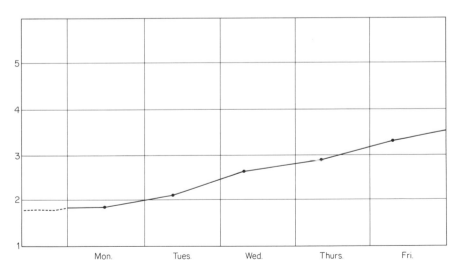

Figure 3.2. Progress chart: clarity of speech. Scale 1–5: 1, inaudible mumbling; 5, clear, audible speech. – – – baseline level of performance; —— trial performance. Assessment at 3 pm daily

difficulties which showed a series of ladders on which the figures of little men could be made to climb up. As the children progressed on their simple task they were able to move the figures up the ladders and entered into this with enormous enthusiasm.

In conclusion, it is clearly the worker's own skills in observing, monitoring and interpreting specific behaviour and in giving feedback which form the most vital element in the assessment and evaluation of the interpersonal skills. To reach an appreciation of what people can achieve at a given time is a capacity which requires time, instruction and practice to develop. It is largely by *doing* that we learn to be effective practitioners, so that the opportunity for practice is vital; this is particularly true of groupwork settings where several clients are being observed at the same time. Observation in the group can, of course, be supplemented by one-to-one sessions, but this is time-consuming and in any case it is often within the setting of a group that the relevant behaviour tends to be displayed. It is therefore enormously valuable to enlist the help and support of group members in monitoring each other's performance and giving feedback and encouragement; this, of course, offers an additional way of checking our own perceptions against other people's. In this kind of work there are, after all, no real experts; we are all amateurs.

SECTION II

Professional skills and how they may be developed

This section is concerned with the specific interpersonal skills needed for professional helping. Observation of social work practice is used to establish the range of professional skills involved and a framework within which they may be considered, while the work of groups of students and practitioners striving to develop their interactive skills provides illustrations of some of the difficulties experienced in developing particular skills and suggests ways of overcoming them.

CHAPTER 4 The skills of professional helping as exemplified by social work

Identifying what Skills are Needed

An activity as complex and demanding as professional helping is necessarily very difficult to conceptualize and any attempt to analyse it into its constituent parts is perhaps even harder. A major preoccupation of the literature has always been to explore and affirm the values underlying professional practice, the aims towards which it should be directed and the relationship between worker and client, as distinct from the actual methods or techniques which may be used to achieve the desired aims. Hence some writers (Wootton, 1959; Brewer and Lait 1980) were able to attack social work theorists on the ground that their discipline was unduly imprecise and their language woolly or grandiose, and even to allege that social workers had no clear idea of what they were doing or how they proposed to do it.

It is, of course, entirely right that we should thoroughly examine the value base of social work and its overall aims before embarking on any attempts at intervention. It is equally right that, once this examination has been rigorously carried out by the profession as a whole and also by workers as individuals, attention should be turned to developing the most effective means of achieving those aims which our value system suggests as most acceptable and appropriate. For individual workers, the "most effective means" involves a high level of practice skills and a good range of techniques for intervention and expertise in liaison with other professionals.

An exhaustive account of the professional skills required for good practice would need to include administrative skills such as the ability to produce clear, accurate reports and records and to manage a demanding and possibly heavy workload. This book, however, is concerned exclusively with *interpersonal* skills, which are in fact much more difficult to specify comprehensively and to classify satisfactorily. What interpersonal skills do social workers need? And are these skills broadly similar, irrespective of the setting in which they are practised, or do medical social workers require a different range of skills from, say, probation officers? One way of pursuing the answers to such questions is to take a definition of the nature and essence of the activity called social work which is widely accepted and to ask what kinds of practice skills such activities demand. Bartlett's *Common Base of Social Work Practice* (1970) offers a definition of social work as focusing upon "social functioning", this being understood to mean "coping behaviour in relation to life tasks and environmental demands". This is a definition which has been widely accepted and could form a useful starting-point for the present enquiry. She goes on, however, to specify *values and knowledge* as the priorities in the development of social work, seeing them, together with focus and orientation, as crucially underpinning intervention; she has almost nothing to say about professional *skills*.

Haines (1975) takes up Bartlett's formulation and goes on to identify the elements of interpersonal intervention as providing, enabling, influencing and creating. This account is still in very general terms, since it is rather a discussion of the activities in question than an analysis of the skills which they demand of workers, but it forms a useful and comparatively simple classification of interaction between worker and client. Butrym (1976) also uses Bartlett's formulation in *The Nature of Social Work* and goes on in a later chapter to describe the social work process as one of "study/assessment/helping/evaluation in the context of a professional relationship" but there is still no exploration of what this might imply in terms of interpersonal skills.

The accounts of interpersonal skills needed in counselling (for instance Egan 1975 and Nelson-Jones 1983) are markedly more restricted in scope than those required in social work, omitting in particular any reference to the giving of information and advice, activities which are clearly important in social work (Goldberg and Warburton 1979).

A further difficulty arises from the fact that most of the literature about the nature and processes of social work and counselling focuses almost exclusively upon the interaction between worker and client. This is particularly conspicuous in Danbury's (1979; 1985) otherwise excellent guide for practice teachers, which focuses entirely on the student's work with clients to the exclusion of any evaluation of liaison and cooperation with colleagues, particularly those in other professions. Yet this is a crucially important area of professional practice, and one on which social workers are having to spend an increasing amount of time. Our own experience of training students has, moreover, repeatedly shown that this is precisely the area of practice in which difficulties are most frequently encountered. When students are asked about the situations which arouse the greatest anxiety in them they are less likely to cite the handling of difficult interviews with clients than various kinds of group situations, whether structured or not, and interchanges with other professionals. Clearly, the interpersonal skills which such situations demand, just as much as the more traditional casework skills, are essential for effective practice, and professional courses need to prepare students for these tasks as well as for direct work with clients. It is essentially basic counselling skills that are needed for face-to-face work with clients, whether the practitioner be a social worker, counsellor, community nurse or therapist. However, the number and variety of other settings in which members of all these helping professions have to work together, and also to establish working relations with people whose professional traditions and attitudes may be very different from their own, mean that they will also require a range of interpersonal skills which are different in kind, and have the character of negotiation or advocacy rather than of interpersonal helping.

Practice Skills—a Programme of Observation

Interest in the problems involved in preparing students for such a range of activities prompted one of us (Mary Collins) to take advantage of a period of study leave to carry out a programme of observations designed to establish as precisely as possible what are the interpersonal skills which social workers are called on to display. The aim was, then, to classify these skills systematically enough to provide material for assessing competence in these areas which could also be used in teaching sequences or in relation to practice in placement or in employment as appropriate. There are several useful existing classifications of interpersonal skills by Egan (1975), Priestley and McGuire (1983) and Argyle (1981), but none of them seemed sufficiently exhaustive to do justice to the full range of social work activities. It thus seemed best to try to establish a new grouping based on the observations; the rest of this second section is based on the grouping which emerged. In the next few pages the singular pronoun "I" will be used, since reference is to the specific research described.

The method best suited to exploring the practice of professional skills seemed to be one of participant observation: I wanted to "sample" the service offered by social workers in the non-statistical sense of the word, rather as a client might sample it. I was able to observe some of the work directly, by being present myself, and indeed also carried out a small amount of work during the period spent with a social services department, where, however, most of my data were obtained by talking to the workers concerned after they had carried out the work. In most cases I was able to do this very soon after (ie within a week), and even when a longer time had elapsed insisted on very specific statements about what was done; no generalizations were accepted.

The first phase of the observation lasted about five weeks and was carried out in a social services area team. It was followed by shorter periods in more specialized settings, two weeks in each of two medical social work settings and one in each of three specialized probation settings—supervision, preparation of social enquiry reports and divorce court welfare. In several instances I "dropped back" on my respondents to gain information on the completion of work which I had seen set in train. It proved difficult to participate in interviews conducted by Social Services workers, whereas in neither the hospital social work nor the probation setting was there any hesitation about involving me nor the least reluctance on the part of clients, even though some of the interviews were extremely tense and complex.

Direct observation has, of course, immense advantages, not least because it is very difficult in interview to make social workers state what they are doing, and how. They will go into immense and (for my purposes) unnecessary detail about the client and her or his history and what she or he says and does, glossing over or omitting entirely what the worker says, so contant questioning is usually required to establish this. No doubt there is a link between this phenomenon and social work's vagueness about the skills required for professional practice.

In addition to collecting information about interviews with clients and carrying a small quantity of work myself, I attached considerable importance to attending a range of other activities in which social workers were involved and which made demands on their interactive skills. These included courts (adult and juvenile), case conferences, case reviews and similar meetings. Such activities occupy a considerable proportion of a worker's time, are as demanding as direct casework, and have in the past been given rather little attention during professional training, though this may well be changing—certainly it has in Exeter. Group situations like these seem to demand many of the skills involved in groupwork as a specialism—something which *as a specialism*, only one of the workers in the area team was involved in (in fact, a social skills group). If, however, as I am suggesting, all social workers are required to display some level of group skills, this would imply that "groupwork" should not be seen as an optional extra in professional training.

In the course of my first weeks of data collection, then, I proceeded to list all the activities I was able to note, "activity" being taken to correspond to what the worker was seen and heard to put into the situation, the nature of her or his intervention, or what she or he reported that activity to be. I continued the list until no more new items were being presented and found that the number had already reached 111, although I was not listing any operations which could clearly be seen to be identical to others already on the list. Classification of this lengthy list proved a matter of considerable difficulty; why this should be the case, how a classification was eventually arrived at and the form which this took will be discussed later.

Because what was being sought was a multifaceted image of social workers' interactive skills and no attempt was being made either to quantify (frequency, etc) or to evaluate (how effectively skills were used), I used a variety of methods other than direct observation to help in the production of material. A simple questionnaire was completed as a pilot study by one social worker in relation to one week's work and again, later, by other members of the team in relation to "a typical day's activities" (or two half-days in some cases). In this questionnaire I used the 9-fold classification of social work transactions devised by Goldberg and Warburton (1979) to focus on what the social worker was actually doing, with the addition of one further category (0) of meetings and discussions with other professionals, but where a single transaction had more than one aspect (information-giving and mobilizing resources, exploratory/assessment and facilitating problem-solving) no attempt was made to identify the most important. I then attempted to analyse the activity in terms of the skills demanded of the social worker, listing them progressively but always checking back with the worker whether I had correctly perceived what she or he was doing and what skill was being used. Later, when I was able to observe a number of interviews directly (mainly in agencies other than Social Services), I still found it important to check back with the worker concerned any perceptions of what she or he had been doing. A number of my respondents commented on the stimulating effect this experience had had on them, by making them much more aware of how they were working.

Other methods of obtaining material included following cases I had seen allocated in team meetings or from office duty and asking informal questions about workers' recent activities.

Lastly, team members were asked specific questions about pieces of work of particular kinds which might be quite demanding but be little represented in the material I was gaining because occurring less frequently. I thus asked about work with families in which there was, or was thought to be, violence, and about case conferences and court attendances. I also enquired about contact with volunteers (as well as with foster parents and child minders) and this confirmed my impression that little work with volunteers was in fact being done. (Later, however, I found it figured much more prominently in probation and in hospital social work.) Specific questions about work with elderly clients were also included; the team had one qualified social worker approaching retirement and a social work assistant both of whom specialized in work with the elderly but other team members also worked with this client group. Knowing that it is common practice for generic teams to give responsibility for work with the elderly to the least qualified staff, I wanted to take a critical look at the assumption that only a low level of skill was required. I found that most of the work with elderly clients was indeed seen as relatively straightforward and undemanding, but that a proportion of it was as difficult and taxing as any social work can be; it is often impossible to judge in advance just how difficult a piece of work is going to be since something which on referral looks quite straightforward can present unforeseen problems and complexities.

Establishing a Classification of Skills Used

Establishing any kind of classification of the skills I observed presented a number of massive difficulties. First, there was the very large number and variety of activities involved; secondly, the difficulty already mentioned which many practitioners experienced in stating what precise skills they were intending to use (as distinct from their overall aim in the situation). I sought the help of six others (two social work lecturers, plus four social workers who had not taken part in the observation side of my research) and presented them with my initial 111 observations, inviting them to group them according to the skill being used. I was confronted by a bewildering array of classifications, and hence the need to find some sort of pattern running through them all. No doubt this was a further manifestation of the difficulty social workers find in thinking in terms of practice skills; some of my helpers were conscious of a continuous pull away from a focus on skill towards classification in terms of the client group or the problem or situation involved. A further source of difficulty lies in the fact that social workers are often doing (at least) two things simultaneously: for instance giving information *and* providing reassurance; supporting and encouraging a client to talk about sensitive topics *and* assessing; confronting a client *and* making plans with her or him. Many apparently simple activities such as information-giving also involved quite complex skills of communicating with a client in terms appropriate to age, capacity or mental state.

One skill observed which seemed both particularly significant and remarkably resistant to classification was the ability to state clearly one's role as a social worker both to clients and to others (such as other professionals). I had noted this skill as being demonstrated in a wide variety of circumstances, and indeed one of my helpers (a medical social worker) established a category for a type of activity which she called "explaining/clarifying the social worker's role". In this category which she placed 23 of my 111 observations, including much interaction with other professionals (explaining clearly the functions, resources and powers of the agency or role of the individual social worker, for instance) and also a number of situations between worker and client (again, explaining the agency's powers but also the management of joint interviews with several family members present and mediation between them—the worker's intervention here being perceived as an expression of professional authority). I was particularly interested to note the frequency with which social workers had to take this kind of stand, as it is something which often causes problems to students in their practice placements and which they find it helpful to work on in simulations. Indeed, this group of skills (which could also be referred to as "impression management") might usefully receive more attention during training.

Another skill element which was readily observable but which ultimately was not classified as a group in its own right was the ability to communicate in terms the client could appreciate, adapted to her or his level of understanding and state of mind. This skill of adapting the method of communication to the hearers and to the situation was encountered in a variety of contexts, one of the most striking being case conferences or reviews where the clients are present and where workers therefore have to present their professional view with the clarity and authority required by the presence of other professionals yet simply enough for the clients to understand, in a situation which is even more stressful for them.

To summarize the difficulties of establishing any simple scheme of classification, then. Social work is a highly complex activity which often requires that different kinds of skill be displayed at the same time. Moreover, the precise situation in which the worker is operating may make demands of its own, involving skills which *may* be seen as a discrete group (though they may resemble skills used in other contexts). Thus, giving a client information and advice about the best means to achieve a desired goal can be seen as similar to the (more directive and controlling) skill used in a family interview to ensure that all members have a fair chance to contribute to the interview, since the family's declared aim is to arrive at a better mutual understanding, but in the actual process of *classification* it was usually found that it was the family group setting that determined how the skill was perceived and categorized. Other skills used in a group setting, however, were obviously identical to skills used in one-to-one: for instance, encouraging members of a mothers' group to see stress and problems as part of normal experience and to talk freely about their own difficulties.

So, rather than a simple system of classification, what emerged from this operation was a *three-dimensional* model of practice skills, comprising not one single family of skills but three such groupings related to and dependent on each other, a formula not dissimilar to that adopted by Butler and Elliott (1985). The three dimensions would then be represented by: counselling skills; skills required by the social work process; skills demanded by particular settings (groups, formal occasions, community work).

Counselling skills
1. Use of the self to establish relationships; reflection, appropriate self-disclosure and communication of accurate empathy to client (or other)
2. Challenging skills; saying "No", avoiding collusion and insisting on reality
3. Reassurance, encouragement and emotional support
4. Helping to promote change; motivating for change, acting with client (or other), reinforcing

Social work processes and stages
5. Assessing and monitoring; questioning, gaining information; evaluation
6. Imparting knowledge and information; giving advice; teaching
7. Planning and setting objectives; collaborating with client, other professionals and volunteers; setting up action systems

Social work in special contexts
8. Group skills: family interviews and mediation; client groups
9. Group skills in stressful situations, such as conferences, courts, multidisciplinary meetings

10. Community skills: negotiation, use of resources, enlist-
ing cooperation

These three dimensions of skill will form the subject of the next three
chapters, but there are first one or two general points to be made.
Some activities (whether in interviews or other forms of interaction)
required a very large range of skills within the period of the interaction, others very few. On the whole, initial interviews demanded
a wide range, while work with long-term clients often involved very
few, perhaps only one or two. Specially structured methods of
working, such as family therapy and social skills training, demanded
a very wide range indeed, drawing on virtually all the groups listed
above; it may be partly because of this that these kinds of work are
experienced as being particularly challenging and tiring.

Many illustrations emerged from my observations of the interrela-
tion of skills from the different dimensions. For instance, the
"process" skill of planning often occurred in combination with the
"counselling" skill of confrontation, where the client was being
challenged to take some action himself to remedy this situation
rather than place the responsibility for this on others. The "process"
skill of assessment also requires the counselling skill of empathy
to ensure that clients' feelings, needs and capacities are fully appreciated, and so do many forms of taking action on behalf of clients,
even where obviously practical arrangements are the principal
concern, so that such arrangements can be adapted to clients'
needs, minimize distress, etc. The need for such a combination of
different orders of skills provides evidence of the difficulty—perhaps
even the impossibility—of designating some kinds of social work
activity (such as the making and execution of practical arrangements) as being simple and straightforward enough to be assigned
to untrained volunteers or social work assistants, unless their work
is very carefully supervised.

It may initially seem odd that the "process" skills of assessment and
planning should be seen as *interpersonal* skills; in fact, this is entirely
appropriate, since assessment and planning ought not, in practice,
to be activities that go on inside the head of the worker but the fruit
of interaction between worker and client. It was a very positive
element in my research that I was actually able to observe this as

a real activity, not simply an ideal to which merely theoretical allegiance was given.

Such a three-dimensional model could, it seems, accommodate all the skills observed, although two people might not necessarily agree as to the dimension which primarily characterized a particular piece of intervention. Though devised originally on the basis of the observation of generic social work carried out in a Social Services area team, it proved equally applicable in other kinds of fieldwork setting. Subsequent observations carried out in two different medical social work and three different probation settings fell unambiguously within the range of interaction which had already been seen in generic social services practice, and could be categorized in the same way.

Differences Between Practice in the Different Settings

It would not be true to say that the demands made by the different settings on workers' interpersonal skills were *identical* in the sense of the same skills being required with similar frequency; emphasis and frequency varied according to the setting, but the same overall repertoire was needed. The differences, moreover, came not *between* specialisms but within them: thus the two weeks spent observing short-term medical social work with geriatric patients involved a lot of collecting and giving of information and joint planning with clients (and often other professionals), whereas the following two weeks spent with a medical social worker responsible for long-term work with families of handicapped children involved a slower pace of work with the emphasis on empathy, realistic reassurance and unobtrusive monitoring of families' coping capacities. Skills of participation in a multidisciplinary team and the presentation of the social work role in this context (the third group) were, of course, much in evidence in both kinds of specialism.

Similarly in probation, a difference in emphasis was noted between what was required for work in the court team (short-term work, again with much collection and giving of information), the team providing supervision (more empathy, and motivating and carrying through change) and the divorce court welfare team (requiring perhaps the greatest variety of skills in a range not dissimilar to that displayed in family therapy). While it is widely held (and my observations confirmed) that less time is spent in the probation setting on providing material and practical help, this fact seems to have no implications for the range and levels of interpersonal skills required; giving practical help could often involve a range of sensitivity and skills at least as extensive as that involved in traditional one-to-one counselling, though the latter is often regarded as a more satisfying and prestigious professional activity.

Fostering the Development of Practice Skills

The wide range of interpersonal skills and the complexity of the combinations in which they have sometimes to be practised renders it a task of formidable difficulty to design a comprehensive programme of training in professional skills. It is simply impossible to predict what will be the demands on a social worker in an unknown situation—and all situations are essentially unknown in advance, since expectations are frequently falsified in the event. Hence flexibility and quickness to adapt are also essential qualities.

Indeed, it may be maintained that flexibility and adaptability are pre-eminently the essential characteristics of good social work. Many of the interpersonal skills identified above are required by other professionals, for whom, however, the variety of skills involved is generally far smaller (Argyle 1981); the distinguishing feature of social work here is the need for such a high degree of versatility and for the ability to alternate, modify and combine. It is ironical that such qualities should be accorded such lowly general esteem. In 1985, for instance, a single advertisement by a London borough invited applications for two posts, one for a qualified generic social worker for the full range of duties, the other for a welfare rights officer requiring no specific qualifications and a range of personal qualities clearly smaller than that needed by the social worker; it was the welfare rights post which carried the higher salary. It seems sad that such generalist abilities should be so lightly regarded in social work. In the medical field, by comparison, there remains something of an imbalance between hospital-based specialisms and general practice, but the general practitioner nevertheless enjoys comparable status and remuneration. In social work, however, the pursuit of career prospects normally involves a shift away from face-to-face work with clients and with it a move towards the exercise of the equally demanding (but arguably fewer) interpersonal skills involved in management (Argyle 1981; Rackham et al 1971).

Implications for Selection and Training

Since it is most unlikely that any single individual will find it equally easy to display a high level of assertiveness when required and a caring and gentle empathetic approach, it follows that anyone entering the caring professions will have much to gain from a sustained endeavour to develop those skills which come less naturally. Skills need to be developed in initial training but they also need to be retained in subsequent practice, and for this to happen there must be continuing opportunities to receive accurate feedback and the ability to receive it and benefit from it. Since, as Rackham et al (1971) point out, "the people most in need of interactive skills training are those who are least capable of extracting accurate feedback in interactive situations", it follows that selection processes must ensure that entrants to the helping professions have the capacity to accept and respond to feedback; but it remains true that responding is not easy, particularly if the feedback is negative, and that some students will find it harder than others. Experience after qualification is likely to increase confidence in one's professional skills, but unless there is also the opportunity for obtaining and learning from feedback these skills will not in fact improve and indeed may actually diminish, so practitioners need to be given ongoing in-service training in these basic skill elements just as much as in more specialized areas of their work.

Interpersonal skills are developed in much the same way as other skills. Like musical skills, for instance, they require both a basis of natural ability and considerable practice; an awareness of any elements in which one is weak with the perseverance needed to improve these; and the knack of combining good technique with genuine feeling—two aspects which are sometimes seen as inimical but are really complementary. Indeed, if I fail to communicate emotion accurately, it may well be my technique which is at fault.

Skills, it needs to be stressed, do not exist on their own, free-floating, isolated from the rest of the practitioner's personality and capacities. They need to rest on a solid foundation of professional values, knowledge and judgement, as well as a commitment to caring at a personal level. What we know and what we believe has profound implications for how we are able to practise our skills. It contributes to an internal dialogue which may disable us, for instance by casting doubt on our objectives or our competence, or may equip us for a skilled performance in difficult circumstances by enabling us to talk our way through it in advance.

In the present book we are not putting forward a package of systematic training in interpersonal skills; there are already some excellent training manuals which include suggestions for exercises starting from a very basic level (see, for instance, Egan 1990, and Priestley and McGuire 1983). Our approach is a more selective one. Taking the three dimensions of skill which we have posited, we shall be looking specifically at the problems which students (and practitioners also) frequently report in attempting to improve their levels of performance. While reference is made to research findings on what clients expect, or feel that they need, from social workers—and sometimes find to be lacking—our main focus is on the difficulties identified and brought to groups which we have run with students and practitioners. Rather than proposing a comprehensive programme, therefore, we are exploring the following questions: what do workers in training (and perhaps after training) find most difficult about this particular group of skills? and how may these difficulties be overcome? It is with these questions that the next three chapters will be concerned.

CHAPTER 5

The counselling skills required in effective professional helping

Many of the skills required for one-to-one work with clients fall under the general heading of counselling skills. They are the skills of creating and using a helpful professional relationship, often under unpropitious circumstances and with people who may be withdrawn, disturbed or hostile; of conveying understanding, empathy, warmth and genuineness; of encouraging and challenging. Further essential skills—which usually do not figure in descriptions of the elements of counselling—include giving information and explanations in a way that is appropriate to the hearer, taking account of such things as age, level of understanding and emotional state, all considerations which make it often quite difficult in practice to give information really well, though in theory information-giving sounds a simple and unproblematic activity. Finally, the ability to give advice when appropriate must also be included, something which is specifically excluded by many writers on counselling. Some professional helpers do indeed work in contexts in which non-directive counselling help is the treatment of choice but for many, including most of those in statutory agencies, the observation that "clients from all backgrounds seem generally oriented towards help that is concrete, directive and supportive" (Rees and Wallace 1982) points to a need to develop and use a fuller range of skills, of which this chapter aims to take account.

Here and in the two following chapters, then, we shall be looking in some detail at the specific interpersonal skills needed by professional helpers. While account is taken of the relevant literature, the discussion will be based mainly on our experience of working with students undergoing professional social work training. This experience is of two kinds: first, that of teaching practice skills in a comprehensive and systematic way; and secondly, running short sequences designed to help students to get to grips with particularly difficult and taxing pieces of interaction. These shorter sequences are necessarily much less systematic, since they are put together from material supplied by participating students as needs and occasion may dictate. They are, however, a more productive source of material for the present discussion as they highlight the elements in social work practice which are frequently experienced as the most difficult. So, while we are endeavouring to take account of the full range of interpersonal skills needed by professional helpers, including some not adequately discussed elsewhere, there will be an inevitable element of imbalance in that more attention will be given to those skills which appear to pose the greatest problems for practitioners, irrespective of whether they are actually required more frequently. More space devoted to a particular skill does not imply that it is seen as more important.

The present chapter is concerned with the skills required in what may be called "relationship work" in general, Chapter 6 discusses the interpersonal skills required by the basic stages in the helping process and Chapter 7 the additional skills which may be demanded by specific kinds of group situations, but it needs to be borne in mind throughout that these different orders of interpersonal skills will be needed in combination and not in isolation. We may consider them in sequence but they cannot be practised so; reality is always likely to call for the three dimensions of skill.

USE OF SELF IN RELATIONSHIPS: ESTABLISHING RELATIONSHIPS; REFLECTION; COMMUNICATING ACCURATE EMPATHY

To say that the importance of the relationship between worker and client is well recognized in the literature is certainly an understatement. Butrym (1976) comments that "So much has been written about the place of the relationship in social work that it is difficult to approach this subject in a way that is not repetitious". In Biestek's classic discussion (1961), the casework relationship is presented as requiring the application of the seven ethical principles seen as essential to casework practice. This relationship has also formed the target for many writers such as Wootton (1959) and Brewer and Laite (1980) who have criticized and denigrated social workers. While it would be difficult to argue convincingly that clients approach helping agencies out of a desire to enter into a meaningful relationship with a professional worker, there is increasing evidence of a correlation between the client's satisfaction with social work help and some elements of this relationship, especially such qualities as friendliness, openness and being easy to talk to: in short, with the effect workers have on their clients and how they make them feel (Rees and Wallace 1982; Collins and Collins 1981; such findings are also applicable to other forms of helping as demonstrated by Truax and Carkhuff 1967).

This stress on the importance of establishing and fostering a warm, understanding relationship carries with it the danger that the worker may concentrate exclusively on doing this, losing sight of the aims of the initial contact. Examples might be cited of child abuse tragedies occurring because the worker was too patient and unassertive, working at developing a relationship with withdrawn or resentful clients, when the need to insist on monitoring the actual state of the child was too urgent to brook delay. Hence the need in training to develop the skills of assertiveness, such as persistence in making enquiries, a subject to which we shall return later. It is sufficient here to stress that it is much easier to be assertive at a later stage of work with the client if the initial contact has been made with complete honesty about its official nature and with no fudging of issues or pretence that the worker is only there as a friend and confidante.

A sense of awkwardness about introducing themselves, their agency and their mission is very common among inexperienced workers and students, so they often benefit greatly from very short role-playing sessions with this as a focus. Familiarity, too, has its dangers; a more experienced worker, well used to making a particular kind of contact, may overlook this need for a clear introduction or fail to realize that the client has not grasped what it is all about. These are some of the things which the worker needs to express in some form at the outset:

(a) I have a good reason for being here
(b) I am John Smith/Sally Jones
(c) I represent/am part of an organization
(d) I may be able to offer help if you need it
(e) I will really listen to what you say to me

The public, and old people in particular, are constantly given warnings not to invite strangers into their homes, so some of the explanations may have to be given on the doorstep (certainly not the easiest of settings!) and may require patience and repetition. While the agency to which the worker belongs and the reason for the call need to be made clear at once, the worker's name is important too, even though the client may well forget it unless it is repeated or written down, since this gives the caller an individual identity. Some students and younger workers experience particular difficulties with point (d)—convincing the client that they may have something to offer. They are easily thrown by responses such as "You're very young, aren't you?", "Have you got any children?" or "How can you understand what it's like to be blind/housebound/black?". They tend to interpret these questions as meaning: "Go away! You're no use to me!", when in fact what the client is really expressing may be rather: "I need help. Convince me that you are someone who can give it!".

How the worker responds at this point may well be crucial to the establishment of an effective helping relationship: often the simple invitation "Well, tell me about it anyway, and we'll see" is not a sufficient response. Additionally, explicit assurances of some kind are often needed that workers, though not in the same present predicaments as their clients, do recognize how difficult and painful the situation is; that they have themselves experienced problems whether directly or at second hand which have helped them to understand what is involved; and that their job is indeed to help with just such difficulties. Some clients particularly welcome assurance of study, training and experience (Rees and Wallace 1982). Lazarus (1971), an American psychologist, cites an entertaining but moving example of a woman patient who cross-questioned him on his qualifications and life experience before she was willing to confide in him. Having in the past abandoned several attempts to seek help from therapists whose practice was to respond to a question by an interpretation or by another question, she was quite overcome by the frankness of his replies and, as Lazarus comments: "The patient learned to trust me during those first few minutes". Later in the same chapter, he cites among the questions which he puts to his trainees after they have carried out an initial interview: "Were you able to provide the patient with legitimate grounds for hope during this interview?". In all helping, the beginning of a good professional relationship rests on the foundation of an understanding, often explicit, about the kinds of help that the worker has to offer.

Clients who are hostile or confused (or both) require particular patience and clarity before a relationship of mutual trust can be established. What, it may be wondered, is the use of role-playing situations such as these? Surely students know quite well that the partner in the role-play is not really angry or confused? This is where the element of feedback is so useful: the partner in the role-play and fellow-students watching it can offer their impressions (perhaps with video playback to contribute evidence) and, by discussing together, the group will be able to establish just what it was that defused the anger of the potential aggressor or made a genuine, direct contact with the confused old person. Equally important, individual students are becoming accustomed by easy stages to situations which make them anxious; habituation in itself tends to diminish anxiety. They can, moreover, be given realistic reassurance about the levels of their performance and be helped not to blame themselves for the limited nature of their success.

Style of Self-presentation

Clearly, with clients like those we have just been discussing, it is particularly difficult to establish rapport; yet it is equally clear how important it is for such a rapport to be established. At this stage, what clients want and need in a worker is probably best summed up in the phrase: someone who is the same, but different. Someone, that is, who has enough in common with them to enter imaginatively into their situation, but is different and separate enough (through professional knowledge and experience) to be able to view it objectively and to bring something fresh to it. The most frequent critical comments which clients make about social workers are that they are (or appear) too young and inexperienced; some criticisms also relate to style of dress and self-presentation (Rees and Wallace 1982). Clients—and also colleagues from related disciplines—often complain about excessive informality in dress, which is sometimes perceived as amounting to scruffiness. Examples of this which we have actually encountered include the following: prisoners on remand smartening themselves up for a visit from their probation officer, only to find that he arrived to see them "looking like something the cat brought in"; a group from the National Association of Young People in Care talking to student social workers in critical terms about the appearance of their own workers; and similar critical comments made by residential workers about fieldworkers attending case conferences. One old lady was so frightened by the appearance of a social worker who was looking for an entrance at the back of her house because she had not answered the front door that she telephoned the police to say that "a gipsy was trying to break into her house".

The image which is presented by the worker must somehow conform to the client's idea of a helping, and helpful, professional if any effective work is to be done. Often, of course, an initial unfavourable impression can be overcome by the worker's caring approach (Simpkin 1978), but it seems perverse to *create* problems which will take time and patience to resolve, especially when these may not be available! There is a clear dilemma here for some students: how to reconcile the need to create a professional image which will convey to the client that quality of genuineness which has been identified as essential to effective helping. This conflict has to be resolved at a cognitive level for many entrants to social work, and this means giving them an opportunity to discuss any negative reactions they may have to the term "professional" and to work out how the concept of professionalism can be purged of its unwelcome associations with the superior, the exclusive and the defensive—in fact the whole idea of a "conspiracy against the laity"—and be redefined as a complex of specialized knowledge and skills which can be used to help the client. It is only workers who have resolved this conflict to their own satisfaction who will be likely to inspire confidence in a wide range of clients. As with so many interpersonal situations, what you believe about yourself, and what you say to yourself about how competent you are and what you have to offer others, are factors which have a crucial influence on your level of performance; simply rehearsing skills and situations will not start to pay dividends until problems in this cognitive area have been resolved. Any course of training for social work and other helping professions therefore needs to make generous provision for explanation and discussion in this area.

Reflection

Reflection figures prominently in most of the literature on counselling: it is typically defined in such terms as "mirroring the verbal and/or emotional content of the client's communication through empathic understanding". The last three words seem to beg an enormous and crucial question: is the worker really communicating to the client that she or he is entering into the client's situation and the client's own feelings about that situation? Many examples of this so-called empathic reflection to be found in the literature leave some room for doubt on this score, especially where reflection takes the form of such simple paraphrases as the following:

> You're uneasy because you're not sure that our sessions will help you manage better but you feel you have to try something (Egan 1975)

> You're confused and finding it difficult to decide what's right for you (Nelson-Jones 1983)

> You're puzzled about what to do (Kadushin 1983)

Comments such as these run the risk of eliciting the response: "But I've just told you that!". It is not surprising, therefore, that the judicious use of reflection is perceived as a matter of some difficulty. It is always important that the worker—and client too—should be aware of why it is being used, and that the worker does not simply resort to it for lack of something more constructive to say.

Simple reflection is an important feature of assessment interviews, and hence also of reassessment and monitoring sessions. If the worker constantly checks back with the client what seems to have been expressed about the current situation and any problems it involves, this offers a major safeguard against misunderstanding and misinterpretation. Feeding back to the client a summary of the various problems brought up at initial interview is an important technique in task-centred work (Reid and Epstein 1972) and also in much behavioural work. "This is what I have understood you to say; have I got it right? Have you any comments to make?" This is particularly valuable in the closing stages of an interview for the preparation of a court report, for instance. In this way assessment can become a joint undertaking between worker and client, not simply something that goes on in the worker's mind as the outcome of the observations made in interview.

What, then, does reflection achieve? Mirrors, it must be remembered, can distort, or they may act selectively. However, if we are alive to such dangers, reflection can be used to check that we have understood correctly what we are being told, and sometimes—it might be more accurate to say occasionally—can make clients aware of patterns in their behaviour, or in things that have happened to them, which they have not previously recognized. It is only fair to say though that there is little evidence that clients find this device particularly helpful or illuminating in resolving their problems.

Self-disclosure

Students and beginning professionals usually feel very unsure how much they ought to tell clients about themselves. It has already been suggested that client confidence is often increased by learning something about the worker's experiences that may link in to the present situation, but such revelations can be excessive and we have also heard complaints from clients who felt that their workers had confided personal problems to them quite inappropriately. So pitching it just right can be a problem.

The most difficult area for many younger professional helpers often concerns their lack of experience, so it is useful for them to work out in discussion just what they might have to offer in terms of personal help to a young single mother or the parents of a difficult teenager. They can then rehearse talking about themselves in simulations, which often produce phrases such as:

"Yes, well, as I haven't any children of my own, I've spent quite a lot of time learning about young children and the problems parents have with them, because my job involves a lot of this kind of thing."

"No, I don't have any children yet, but my training has helped me to understand what's involved and how difficult things can be."

Students are often reluctant to mention their training to clients, yet the latter seem to value it (Rees and Wallace 1982) and surely the acknowledgement that workers need to be trained is evidence that clients' problems are being taken seriously, an appreciation of the fact that life is actually quite difficult and complex and that we professionals ought therefore to do our homework before we try to help people through it. To act otherwise is to diminish the seriousness of their predicament, and to say in effect that it is really all so easy that anyone could sort out situations of this kind—anyone, that is, except someone as inept as these clients of ours. So the message the client really needs to hear will be something along the lines of:

"Yes, I am quite young and I haven't been in the same situation myself, but I have learned/heard something about it, and I can imagine how difficult/painful it must be—won't you tell me more about it?"

After all, it is usually the client who is the real expert about the situation.

One particular fact about themselves which some workers and students may find specially difficult to disclose to clients is their own marriage breakdown. Two divorced women in a student group we were running discussed with other members their anxiety about clients possibly questioning them in this area and worked out a way of dealing with the challenge this offered them, role-playing a scene in which an imaginary client, seeking help with her own marital problems, questioned the worker about her marital status. The kind of response evolved was along the following lines:

"I have been married, but I'm divorced now. Even though things didn't work out for me, I think I've learned a lot from it."

Whatever the form of the client's actual question may be, what is often really being asked is, what sort of person are you, and how can I be sure that I can trust you? Fudging or evasion in the face of this question can be extremely damaging. Most clients will resent "a response growing out of defensiveness" (Truax and Carkhuff 1967), whereas a worker "who has learned not to be afraid of himself does not have to create an image of himself that denies how he actually feels" (Keith-Lucas 1972).

Accurate Empathy

There can be no doubt that the ability to convey accurate empathy lies close to the heart of any truly creative helping relationship. Perhaps it would be better to paraphrase the term as: the ability to communicate to people that we have really understood how they are feeling. The element of "appreciation" needs stressing: to give real help, you must not only identify another's feelings correctly but realize what experiencing those feelings means for that person in terms of intensity, consequences, conflicts with other emotions or sense of duty—and somehow express your appreciation of all these factors. Much attention has been given to the communication of empathy in the literature on counselling, yet a great deal of what is cited as examples of "appropriate response" is mere reflection, and mere reflection is not empathy. For instance, the formula (it is virtually that) put forward by Nelson-Jones and Egan: "You feel. . . because. . ." is simply reflecting, with the addition of a label for the emotion involved. Sometimes, moreover, the worker's response misses the mark by underestimating the strength of the feeling involved, as well as by the failure to add any expression of comprehension. Two examples from Kadushin (1983):

> *Mrs Y*: So when the doctor said I needed the operation and I knew I had to go to the hospital, I thought, what am I going to do with the kids? who will take care of them I mean, there's nobody. Half the people, like relatives, I know, are too far away, they can't come.
> *Worker*: You feel all alone.

> *Interviewee*, to a worker who was trying to explore why she felt upset about her decision to break away from her church: I'm afraid of going to hell.
> *Worker*: That can be upsetting.

This last, if read out to a group of students, can be relied on to raise a gust of laughter; it is so grotesquely inadequate to the intensity of the client's anxiety.

If simply labelling the client's emotion is unlikely to help, what more is needed? Role-plays can usefully explore this, especially if they are interrupted at a point where the "client" is clearly not feeling understood and the question is put to the "client": "What do you need from the worker now?". Alternatively, the "worker" and any others present during the role-play can volunteer and review a range of suggestions. At such crucial points, where the client is wondering whether to trust the worker and whether she or he is likely to be of any help, the worker may need to go well beyond the mere recognition of the client's feelings and to explore their causes and their implications—even if up to that point the worker has been primarily a passive listener and the client has been talking freely. The conventional phrases like "It must be very distressing for you that your daughter has been born handicapped" are not enough; something like the following might be more appropriate:

"I can imagine how shattering it must be for you, after all the excitement of waiting for your first child—you never expect anything like this to happen to *you*. It's such a shock—it takes a long time to realize it, really to take in what's happened, doesn't it?"

Most of all, what a client in this situation will probably most need to explore is the uncertainty about what the future will hold, especially as medical staff often genuinely do not know the answers to questions about how the child will develop and therefore tend to brush them aside; hence the need for someone else to share some of the discomfort of this uncertainty with the client.

Similarly, a response to a harassed parent such as "You get bad-tempered with the children at times", which is a simple paraphrase of what the client has just said, needs more elaboration along the lines of, "I can understand that you get bad-tempered with the children at times, but it must be very difficult when you're on your own with them", or ". . . and you must feel really bad about it afterwards". If the right note has been struck, it often draws a reply from the client such as "Yes, that's it exactly!"—an indication that this person really does feel understood. Such a clear recognition that you have got it right does not come often, but sensitivity and awareness will often detect less explicit (possibly non-verbal) expressions of the same appreciation.

CHALLENGING SKILLS: AVOIDING COLLUSION AND INSISTING ON REALITY

Good professional practice will inevitably involve, on occasion, pointing out to clients things which they would probably prefer to ignore and insisting on facts which all concerned (workers as well as clients) would like to leave cloaked in comfortable vagueness. This requires the challenging skills recognized and described in the counselling literature but, in addition, many helpers carry an investigative or controlling function not required of a counsellor and demanding a capacity for assertiveness and the constructive use of authority which counselling itself seldom or never requires. This can be a particularly difficult area for people whose choice of profession arises from the compassionate impulse to help those in distress and difficulty, but it may be useful to remember that the Latin root of the word "compassionate" which gives us "passive" and "patient" also provides "passion" and "passionate". The accent is always on feeling: not only on experiencing feelings, but also acting out their expression. We know, moreover (Sainsbury 1975; Rees and Wallace 1982), that clients generally do not find the passive, ever-patient, all-accepting social worker helpful; passivity tends to be seen as lack of concern.

Confronting clients in the ways to be discussed here can often give rise to an ethical problem for the worker: if we say that we believe in self-determination, how can we justify imposing our views of reality and of reasonable behaviour on someone else? This is a question of great importance and difficulty which there is no space to discuss at length here, and one which in fact concerns the entire issue of forms of social (or indeed medical) intervention which are not actively sought.

Essentially, what the worker is expressing to the client in the form of a challenge can actually be seen as a form of affirmation of the individual right to decide for oneself, saying in effect: It's your life! It's for you to face its real difficulties and decide for yourself how you will tackle them. There is a curious irony in the popular stereotype of welfare workers as interfering busybodies imposing their own standards and beliefs on hapless clients, seen as unwilling recipients of advice and guidance, whereas, in practice, workers frequently find themselves having to resist clients' pressure to "decide for me" or "tell me what I ought to do".

Akin to the issue of refusing to take on the clients' responsibility for making their own choices is that of challenging the false assumption that they are powerless to change their situation. Certainly people are powerless to change anything unless they really believe they can. This sense of powerlessness may be expressed in various ways: perhaps in simple apathy and dejection, or possibly by playing one of the games described by Berne (1968) such as "Why don't you

—Yes, but", in which every suggestion advanced by the helper for improving things is countered by some insuperable objection from the client. Memories of clients who are adept at playing this particular game can haunt us years later. Phil, for instance, described in a training session how he had made a succession of arrangements for an elderly client, Annie, to be admitted to a home, only to find repeatedly that she cancelled them at the last minute, usually on the very morning of the day she was due to go to the home for a trial period; this despite the fact that it had all been discussed with her at length and she had emphasized that it was what she wanted. Yet here she was, after the fourth such reversal, saying "It's just not suitable" and managing to make Phil feel guilty (both in real life and afterwards in role-play with a fellow-student), so that he was virtually excusing himself for not having done a better job and behaving as though the breakdown in arrangements was his fault.

This example highlights the two stages required in our response. The first stage is to try to arrive at an objective view of the situation. How realistic is the client being? Have I really done all that was possible or appropriate? Does the client really need to face these things which are being denied or evaded? A decision on the need for confrontation may involve several questions of this kind, although it sometimes has to be made very quickly indeed. Clearly, in the situation just described, Phil has to make some kind of challenge or he will find himself manipulated into further fruitless activities of the same kind, but he has to remind himself of the answers to some of the relevant questions. Yes, she is playing games with me. Yes, I did offer her several alternatives of the kind she said she wanted. Yes, I do have to face her with this. Role-play then offers the opportunity of experimenting with different forms of confrontation, the choice between them being determined by Phil's personal style, by his relationship with Annie and by Annie's own background and personality. It could be anything from: "Come off it, Annie, you aren't playing fair! You're just having me on!" to: "Look, Mrs Forbes, this is really not getting us anywhere", but it would certainly have to include, in some form of words, a close comparison between what she had expressed a wish for in the past and what had actually been offered; all this moving on to a possibility that Annie will look again at what she does want and either make a serious decision for an option previously dismissed or else redefine what it is she wants.

Setting out clearly to clients what workers' powers are, and what are the limitations and constraints upon the help they can give, is another form of confrontation which can be experienced as quite difficult, especially by younger workers. To insist to parents who are telling the worker to "Go away and mind your own business" that "I do have the right to see your child—so please will you show me where she is?" is a typical example of such a situation. Another is that recorded by Keith-Lucas (1972; writing in the USA, where social work and probation are entirely distinct and separate):

> I recently had occasion to teach a number of adult probation officers. Before we began I was apprehensive about their reactions to being instructed by a social worker. . . I thought they would find my material on empathy very hard to take but that they would have very little difficulty with reality. Exactly the reverse was true. These men were willing to go to all lengths to try to understand their probationers, and to do things for them. . . The one thing they found almost impossible to do was to tell them that they were on probation and that if they broke its conditions the judge could and might send them to prison. Yet it was around this fact that they could have given the greatest help. If, that is, they had used this fact not as a threat but as a reality with which the probationer needed help.

In order to be able to confront clients in this way, workers need to have thought through their own position as representatives of their agency, and to be convinced that it is their right—indeed their duty —to intrude, if necessary, into situations such as these. Again, therefore, it is often helpful to have some discussion of the basis and justification for intervention before a role-play is embarked upon. Anyone who is unclear or hesitant about the position to be taken up and the basis on which it rests will not be able to state it with clarity and conviction, and will either adopt a very authoritarian and rigid manner or else will fudge crucial issues. An example which can often crop up at an early stage in a child care referral is the parents' anxious question: "Can you take him away? Are you going to?". It is only too tempting to respond with a quick, uncritical reassurance, and it requires much more confidence to reply honestly: "Yes, I do have the power to take children into care if there's good reason to be worried about them, but as long as you're able to go on looking after him all right I certainly shouldn't want to do that with Johnny".

This proviso "as long as things continue satisfactorily" certainly needs to be added, even though clients may choose to forget it, for it is a potent source of complaint by parents whose children have been removed that the worker "always said he wouldn't do it". Lack of the courage required to state unpalatable truths or insist upon the discussion of vital but embarrassing or distressing topics can lead to disastrous consequences and, with some justification, can be seen by clients as a betrayal.

Challenging skills of this and similar kinds figure prominently among those situations which both students and experienced workers find particularly difficult to handle, and while the need for confrontation is recognized in much of the literature on counselling, the practice of social work is likely to entail some form of confrontation with the client more often, and in a wider variety of situations, in view of its investigative and authority functions. It may be useful to close this section with a list of some such situations which students and practitioners may find it useful to consider and to rehearse, in view of the difficulties which they often report with them and the disastrous consequences which may flow from an inability to exercise the appropriate skills. These include:

- Disclosing unpalatable facts, such as a court decision to a family member not present, or a social services decision not to allow parental access to a child in care or not to accept a couple as foster parents;
- Stating the authority of your agency and yourself as representing it, for instance warning a probationer of the consequences of failing to report or a parent of the consequences of abandoning a child;
- Insisting on such authority in the face of denial or evasion;
- Challenging the accuracy or veracity of a client's statements (eg when preparing a social enquiry report);
- Resisting attempts by a client to "get you on his side" in the face of authority, or against another family member;
- Facing people with patterns in their behaviour and with the consequences which flow from it;
- Challenging stereotyping processes, as when a parent sees

one child as all good and another as all bad, and thinking and behaviour influenced by prejudices such as sexism and racism;

- Challenging negative patterns of thinking, especially with anxious or depressed clients—their need to be perfect, their perception of minor misfortunes as major calamities, their readiness to predict disaster;
- Challenging apathy and passivity, such as the excuses "I'm sick, so I don't have to think about it" or "It's not my fault—things just happen to me and I can't do anything about it".

This list is, of course, not exhaustive—no such list could be—but it can serve to alert us to the crunch element in a variety of situations which do occur remarkably frequently in everyday practice.

REASSURANCE, SUPPORT AND ENCOURAGEMENT

The notion of "support" as a helping activity has often been criticized as being vague and woolly, and as referring to a type of activity which might undermine rather than enhance clients' capacities to do things for themselves. What we are concerned with here is, however, very different from this traditional notion of support; indeed in some ways it has more in common with confrontation, in that it involves a positive input into the client's experience. It is a truism to say that many clients have poor self-images, and the purpose of the skills we are now considering is to challenge and transform these images. The expression "making people feel *affirmed*" is sometimes used to describe the process of enabling them to feel more confident, stronger, more positive about themselves; few aspects of helping activity are more valuable.

Reassurance about externals is another aspect of the same function: helping people to see that their worst fears and imaginings are not justified. It is, of course, essential that such reassurance be absolutely realistic. It is of no use to say "It will be all right" with apparent certainty when there is a chance that things may actually go wrong, but it would be most unfortunate if a small degree of uncertainty were to prevent a worker from reassuring clients that the steps which had been (or were to be) taken gave them the best possible chance of success. Indeed, truly accurate empathy will often reveal that a client is entertaining a number of quite unjustified apprehensions about future catastrophes, believing, for instance, that others pose a threat which is actually quite unrealistic, and the correction of such misapprehensions is a valuable form of reassurance. An insensitive worker might not realize that the client was experiencing these fears, or would not spend the necessary time and effort in demonstrating their groundlessness. Much information-giving (a subject to which we return in the next chapter) is designed to alleviate anxiety rather than provided in response to any direct request for knowledge: a typical example of this would be the probation officer collecting information for a social enquiry report but spending time and effort also on explaining to the client what could be expected to occur at the next court appearance.

Research material provides ample evidence of the importance of offering positive support and reassurance to clients, often from the very outset of work. It seems clear that workers consistently underestimate the degree of anxiety which clients experience, especially at the initial contact. Reassurance offered at this stage is particularly appreciated; Rees and Wallace mention specifically the assurance that the client is valued as a person, and has no need to be ashamed at seeking help. Often, too, clients feel isolated in their predicament, as though there must be something odd, sick or deserving of blame in what they are experiencing or what they have done; frequently this is by no means the case, and they need to be told so. Much of the criticism of social workers as too passive, just sitting back and listening and giving nothing back, may arise from the absence of just this kind of response.

Lishman (1978), in a revealing and admirably honest follow-up study of her own clients, found that the files on those clients who expressed dissatisfaction with the service she had given them showed an emphasis in her work upon problems and confrontation, with no reference to valuing the clients and supporting their strengths; with the satisfied families, on the other hand, work had included valuing and supporting as a specific goal. Of course, there is a danger here in the too easy acceptance and application of such findings, possibly giving rise to a cosy and comfortable atmosphere in which nothing is changed in the client's situation and problems because no unpleasant realities are ever confronted, so the client is given nothing but the soothing and fallacious message that every-thing is all right really. This is a very real danger but it must not be allowed to lead us into focusing exclusively on negative, problematic elements in clients' situations or to make us forget to give very explicit verbal expression to those abstract notions of warmth and acceptance essential to effective helping. Sainsbury et al (1982) also note that the client's valuation of encouragement seems to be underestimated by probation officers. For this reason it may be necessary to draw the attention of students and beginning workers —and perhaps some more experienced workers too—to the impor-tance of recognizing and responding to their clients' needs for reassurance and approval. It is all too easy to overlook such needs, as Lishman concluded she had done with some of her clients.

It is certainly worth while to explore ways of refining and develop-ing this important skill. One simple exercise involves pairs of students in which A talks to partner B about something in her or his recent experience which is proving worrying or upsetting. B's task is to respond to this in a way which recognizes the reality of A's anxiety or distress but also starts to explore ways of resolving it. A then provides feedback on what was found helpful in B's responses. For workers and more experienced students, it may be more produc-tive to take on the role of clients who are prey to excessive anxiety or distress (perhaps someone they have worked with); they can then explore in twos or threes which kinds of responses seem to help the most.

HELPING TO ACHIEVE CHANGE: MOTIVATING AND ACTING WITH CLIENTS; REINFORCING

The extent to which professional helping is intended to bring about change, and is effective in so doing, is a matter for some debate. Pincus and Minahan (1973) put their main emphasis on change and indeed refer to the social worker as a "change agent"; on the other hand, Davies (1981/1985) sees this element as almost periph-eral and the social worker as a maintenance mechanic, oiling the wheels to keep the system turning over smoothly. The same debate between the concepts of change and maintenance may be conduct-ed in relation to the work of the community nurse, the occupational therapist or the doctor. A number of studies of the "effectiveness" of social work intervention (eg Fischer, 1976) might be cited as evidence of its failure to bring about measurable, tangible and objective change, but it is arguable that the criteria for change adopted in these studies are too crude and simplistic and that it is quite possible that something was being achieved which was recognized as valuable by both the workers and the clients.

It seems clear from some of the research, such as the study by Goldberg and Warburton (1979), that while researchers themselves may give the effectiveness of social work a low rating, practitioners are somewhat more positive in their view of the service they give and what it can achieve but are still quite critical of it, whereas the clients are the most satisfied of all. This is clearly a generalized finding in a very complex area, since it involves the ideas of satisfaction, helping and change, which are clearly interrelated though they do not coincide. It may be useful, however, to refer to another study by Goldberg (1970) in which comparison was made between two groups of elderly people, one receiving the standard welfare service (occasional visits by unqualified welfare staff with enormous caseloads and no supervision) and the other being visited by qualified staff with small caseloads and regular supervision. While the outcomes differed little between the two groups on the more clear-cut criteria, such as the proportions who had survived or died during the period of the study or the numbers still living independently versus those receiving residential or nursing care, when it came to the subtler, less dramatic criteria such as involvement in various social activities and the way the clients evaluated themselves and their life situation, there was a clear difference in favour of the group who had received the special service; old people in this group tended to be more active and to see themselves and their lives in much more favourable and positive terms. These are indeed changes, and important ones for the people concerned, and it may well be that most of the changes that a community social service can bring about will be no more dramatic than these. Certainly our own recent research identified many pieces of social work in which change seemed to be a central feature, and indeed it was to be identified by the workers who helped to classify the observations.

The first stage in promoting change, and often the most difficult, is motivating the client to attempt it. Keith-Lucas (1972) among others has drawn attention to the resistance often encountered when offering people help designed to change their present situation; hence an explicit recognition of the feeling of hesitancy and reluctance experienced by many clients is likely to be an appropriate starting point. The device known as "paradox therapy" involves the therapist actually pushing in the same direction as the resistance in order to disturb the existing equilibrium, rather than pushing against the resistance and thereby possibly increasing its strength. People are also often reluctant to envisage changes because they simply cannot believe that any change is really achievable, so careful work may be needed to share with the client what change is possible and how it might be achieved. It is especially useful here if the worker knows of any similar achievements by the same client in the past which can be used as evidence that success is not impossible. Finally, perhaps the most potent element in building up the motivation is exploring what the payoff for change might be, what advantages might realistically follow. There may be drawbacks, too, which will also need considering.

The skills of encouraging people to contemplate change and helping them to achieve it are seldom used on their own; far more often they need to be combined with skills of challenge and reassurance. Quite a lot of pain and discomfort can also be involved, especially in situations where people have the necessity for change thrust upon them, by bereavement or physical incapacity for instance. External constraints like shortage of time or resources put increased pressure on the worker. Mrs Briggs, an 80-year-old patient in an acute hospital ward, had suffered a stroke and could neither remain in hospital nor return to her home; her social worker sensed her reluctance to consider other plans. This is a familiar problem in hospital social work. Ideally, the worker would have liked several weeks in which to work around and through the subject gradually, clearly not a realistic expectation in the hospital setting, but at least she was able to see her client repeatedly at short intervals and from the outset she recognized both the client's reluctance and the absolute necessity for making some agreed plan for the future. Sometimes, however, the time-scale for such work can be greatly lengthened. Mr and Mrs Scott, for instance, needed to think about what possible future changes were to be made in the living arrangements for their daughter, who suffered from spina bifida and for whom they had cared for many years, granted that she now wanted to live away from home and had some prospect of doing so, though she was severely handicapped and her parents had been in the habit of doing everything for her. In this kind of long-term work, the prospect of change can recede so far into the future that parents and worker collude in never discussing it at all, until perhaps some disaster like the carer's illness precipitates a change which, being hasty, is unlikely to be adequately discussed and planned. Workers may feel diffident about obtruding delicate and potentially painful subjects on their clients' notice, but they need to ask themselves whether in a particular case this arises from their belief in the client's inherent right to self-determination or from their own lack of confidence. Equally, most can benefit from practising in role-play the difficult combination of skills required to bring clients to the point of contemplating inevitable changes or an uncertain or unattractive prospect, while remaining themselves gentle, sympathetic and caring.

It is often said of methods of work based on behaviour modification that they will not be effective unless the client is really motivated to change anyway, a proviso which in fact applies equally to all methods of promoting change. For all sorts of reasons workers, like their clients, are tempted to accept the *status quo*; both parties may find it easier to play "Ain't it awful!" (Berne 1968). Moreover, if you don't try anything, then you don't run the risk of failure. Getting stuck in such ways is an all too familiar experience. Students and workers practising the difficult transition from the level of empathy and a sympathetic assessment of the client's situation to a more active one where change can actually be envisaged and carried forward often find it helpful to make a distinct change in their physical posture and their manner of speech, perhaps leaning forward and speaking more incisively, signalling a kind of "gear change" to themselves as well as the clients.

It is increasingly recognized that working out and agreeing specific tasks which clients then complete as steps towards their designated goal is a valuable and effective means of promoting change. Here, the worker's skill lies in the selection of tasks and encouragement —choosing tasks which are within client's capacities and convincing them that they do have the ability to complete them—but it is often an additional source of encouragement if the worker engages to complete some other task at the same time.

The Teaching of Skills

Responsibility for the course of change rests more squarely on the worker where various forms of teaching are involved: teaching life skills such as budgeting, for instance, or social skills training. It can be important for the worker to be able to model behaviour for the client, such as parenting behaviour or social interaction, but workers are often reluctant to offer themselves as models in this way, perhaps through modesty or a fear of intrusiveness. Demonstrating cooking skills seems to raise no problems, but demonstrating interpersonal skills seems somehow presumptuous. Workers who have themselves experienced during their training how helpful modelling can be are likely to feel less diffident about using it themselves, since a brief demonstration is often much more effective than a lengthy explanation and far more memorable. Most memorable of all is the actual rehearsal either by the client or by client and worker together of what is being learned—evidence of the truth of the saying: "What I hear, I forget; what I see, I understand; what I do, I remember". Most of the third section of the present book is concerned with this vivid and creative form of learning.

With many clients who are depressed and apathetic, a lot of encouragement and energy are required to get things moving in this way, and some students and workers are reluctant to make any approach which involves giving explicit instructions to the client such as "Try it this way" or "Try taking a different line". This seems to them intrusive, and they will sometimes in discussion make comments such as "We don't have the right to tell clients how to live their lives/bring up their children". This block to their learning needs to be tackled on two levels: first, on a cognitive level, by exploring the role of workers in offering whatever problem-solving strategies are appropriate to people who are actually suffering because their own coping mechanisms do not meet their needs; and secondly by experiencing just how helpful, and hence welcome, such coaching is seen by their clients to be. This latter can be demonstrated in simulation by getting the "worker" to exchange roles and take on that of a parent, while someone else role-plays a worker being first sympathetic but passive and then active and directive, offering professional advice and suggestions in a non-threatening way. It is then readily seen why clients typically prefer the active worker to the passive and why the refusal to give any practical advice is actually resented.

Reinforcement

The problem about reinforcement is not that it is difficult to give, but that it is so easy to forget. The simple words "Great! Well done!" mean so much to a struggling client and we are so niggardly about using them. If suitable reminders are given when necessary during training, workers will be able to internalize the vital message: tell people when they have got things right.

It is this group of change-oriented skills for which the establishment of a secure foundation in the professional's view of her or his role and competence is the most crucial. Nineteenth-century social workers were quite clear about their right, and indeed their duty, to intervene to bring about change in other people's lives, and no doubt this is a major reason why they were so often effective in such adverse circumstances. In recent years, however, questions have been raised as to whether anyone, social worker or other, has the right to try to change anyone else. Yet it remains a fact that many, perhaps most, of our clients are in states of perplexity, confusion and distress which they desperately want to bring to an end; so desperately that they may actually themselves be willing to change in order to do this.

CHAPTER 6   Interpersonal skills required for basic helping processes

The interpersonal skills discussed in the previous chapter are, clearly enough, central to professional helping, but considered in isolation, without any particular context, they supply only a single dimension of that practice. A second dimension is supplied by the basic processes of assessment, information-giving and planning, which, if they are to be shared with the client, cannot simply be regarded as events occurring inside the worker's head, but involve their own proper group of interpersonal skills. Again, the same will apply to the skills demanded of other workers such as occupational therapists and community nurses, for whom the assessment of clients' situations, specifically including how these situations look and feel to those who are in them, is a central part of their professional activity. We have discussed assessment methods elsewhere (Collins and Collins 1981; also in Chapter 3 of the present book, with specific reference to social skills training). Here, however, our concern is to try to pinpoint difficulties which interaction with clients may raise for workers trying to carry out assessment, communicate information or work out a plan of action; and also to offer some suggestions for countering these problems. No helping activity ought to be seen as an arbitrary intervention by a self-sufficient expert operating in isolation; rather it should be conceived and executed as a piece of collaboration carried out jointly by clients and professionals. This element may actually make it more demanding in terms of the worker's interpersonal skills, since many clients may find it easier to understand the role of someone who comes into their life to make a detached professional judgement than that of a worker whose function is more that of an enabler or a catalyst, empowering them to make their own decisions and resolve their own problems.

INTERPERSONAL SKILLS USED IN ASSESSMENT, MONITORING AND EVALUATION

Assessing, monitoring and evaluating are activities which are so clearly related that it is logical and natural to view the interpersonal skills which they involve as a single group, whether practised at the beginning or end of the intervention or at an intermediate stage. In some ways, the initial assessment can be the most demanding in terms of interpersonal skills, since virtually all the material concerned is by definition new; at this point we, for our part, have no specific knowledge about what kind of approach would be most acceptable to the client or what kinds of topics are best avoided initially. Clients may find it a new and possibly strange experience to meet a professional helper or they may have been antagonized by unfortunate episodes in the past, and in either case they may well not welcome this attention. So, while some may be so eager to talk about their problems that they respond immediately and willingly to opening enquiries, there will be others who will need encouragement and reassurance before they reveal what is troubling them. Above all, they need to be convinced that the person listening has some real help to offer.

The question of confidence applies in both directions, moreover: even though the client may trust the worker, can the worker trust the client and accept as true, or at least as valid, what s/he has to say? And ought the worker to share with the client at this stage all the relevant information which has been obtained from other sources about the client and her or his situation? Ideally, one would like to answer all these questions in the affirmative, but there are occasions when the worker will feel bound by confidentiality not to reveal some of this information, something which may well hamper the development of mutual trust. A typically delicate situation arises when family members are seen individually in succession. Establishing the conditions about what will be withheld from subsequent work with other family members and what it may be useful for all concerned to share is a priority item on the agenda of many initial interviews, often needing discussion at the outset and reaffirmation at the conclusion. There are temptations for the worker either to overlook the issue and omit any discussion of these controlling conditions or to take a simplistic approach which stresses the confidentiality aspect to the extent of maintaining absolute secrecy as between interviews with different family members. This last, however, has the serious disadvantage of undermining, perhaps even destroying, the potential the worker would otherwise have for a mediating role. The ability to explain to an adolescent who is feeling alienated from his parents how much loving concern his mother has been expressing towards him in his absence is too valuable to lose, when it is so easy in everyday family life for the expression of this concern to be crowded out by the parental nagging and sniping which anxieties so often generate. Where difficulties in family relationships are concerned, it is usually best to be honest about the fact that one view of the situation has been heard from another family member but without giving any details, going on to say something like "And now I'd like to hear your view of things" in a way that expresses willingness to hear someone else's viewpoint on the subject with an open mind.

Even where the conflicting viewpoints of different family members are not involved, the question can still arise: how much confidence can be placed in the accuracy or veracity of what a client is telling us? A social worker can seldom afford to be quite like the "credulous therapist" of personal construct theory (Epting 1984), whose central concern is to enter into the world of the client and see it through her or his eyes, and yet a real assessment process will always include some element of this. Thus, even though the worker may be convinced from direct observation that Jason is no naughtier than the average 13-year-old, the fact that his mother regards him as being rude, disobedient, disruptive and generally impossible to handle is part of her reality. Such a perception might need to be challenged at a later stage, but at the point of initial assessment it will probably be sufficient to note it, and perhaps to ask for some clarification or some actual incidents that support this view: "What does he do?", "When did this happen last?" or "What is it you find most difficult?", for instance.

Assessment, at the intial stage in particular, is much concerned with the gathering of information, and hence involves asking a lot of questions. In writings about counselling a frequent distinction is made between "closed" and "open" questions. A closed question is one which anticipates a simple, often single-word answer such as "yes" or "no" which does not offer any way of continuing or taking further the conversation. In most forms of counselling such closed questions are usually avoided in favour of the less precise, more open invitation ("Tell me more about how you. . ."), but they are often essential at the beginning of assessment and their avoidance can result in failure to collect basic factual data. If, however, the interchange remains in that form it will eventually stagnate. Indeed, an interview can sometimes become "bogged down", with minimal participation by the client, precisely because the worker is conducting it purely on the basis of closed questioning, thereby enabling the client to limit replies to monosyllables.

The client who "won't talk", won't give back anything even when given the utmost opportunity by open questions, presents special problems for the worker. Such a client may, even when asked unstructured questions designed to help him talk about his feelings towards his family, his job or his mother's attitude towards his girl-friend, merely respond "OK", "Dunno" or "All right". This is a useful familiar situation for a role-play which enables workers to experiment with different kinds of approach without the frustration of the actual interview situation. One approach which can be helpful is to invite the client to talk *quite precisely* about some topic which you have reason to think is of some concern to him. "Yes? Well, tell me what happened when you went home with your girl-friend last night. . . What did your mother say?. . . and what did you do?". The way such questions are worded can be important. Questions beginning "Why. . ." are often experienced as threatening (Keith-Lucas, 1972, for instance, recommends that they be avoided altogether) and there is an important difference in effect between asking "Why did you do that?" and "What made you do that?" although the meaning may be almost identical.

Initial assessments contain by definition an element of novelty which is usually sufficient to keep workers "on their toes" but later, where assessment has become monitoring, it is all too easy, especially under the pressure of a heavy workload, to slide into a routine series of automatic questions such as "How are you then? Job all right? Family OK? Right, see you in a fortnight's time then". It would take an assertive client to respond: "Well, there are some other things you should know about," or "I'm not too happy about the way things are going there and I'd like to talk to you about it". Tom, a member of one of our social skills groups, actually asked to role-play raising a new subject with his social worker; she had a good relationship with him and was monitoring his seemingly stable situation but had not realized that there was a fresh subject he wanted to discuss with her but lacked the skills to raise.

An important part of assessment and evaluation will usually be checking back our own perceptions with clients. Useful initially for checking the accuracy of assessments, it can have an added usefulness at a later stage when progress has been made and this progress can be firmly underlined—something which is good for the morale of worker and client alike. It is all too easy to dwell on failures.

Feeding back to the client in this way our conclusions about the point which she or he has reached can comprise a "summary that helps the client understand himself more fully and see the need for action" (Egan 1975). Used at the start of a subsequent interview, it can help to prevent the client from repeating what was brought to the last interview; and it can always convey an invitation to move on, to consider what might be done next, witness Egan's view of "summarizing as a bridging response"—that is, the response of recognizing what are the problems in the present situation, implying at the same time that something might be done about them. The question, expressed or clearly implied, "And where does that lead us?" needs to follow a full discussion of the client's situation and how she or he feels about it if there is any prospect of helping the client to bring about any change in it.

A similar need to hold the right balance between different modes of communication emerges from Reid and Epstein's discussion (1972) of what they call "systematic and responsive communication", two elements between which there is often, perhaps usually, a certain degree of tension. The systematic element is required to ensure that all necessary areas of concern, all problems and needs, are adequately explored and neither they nor any possible source of help or support is overlooked; the responsive element lies in the equally essential ability to attune oneself to the feelings and anxieties of the client. The task-centred approach to casework makes this tension quite explicit, because the client's feeling of anxiety and urgency about a particular problem and emotional commitment to tackling it are crucial to the selection of the target problem, which is, by definition, the one on which the client will be most motivated to work. At the same time, the worker has to be disciplined and systematic in order, for instance, to identify precise tasks and assess how feasible these are and how directly related to the target problem.

For training sessions, situations can readily be devised, whether imaginary or based on actual cases, in which students or workers can practise and develop an appropriate balance between systematic and responsive styles, or between closed and open questioning. This is a particularly important piece of skills training, since without it people run the risk of simply developing their own personal style in the way that suits them best, without giving any thought to how they may need to change it or depart from their usual style to meet the needs of a given client. In these training role-plays, however, they can develop adaptability and flexibility. Some minor difficulties may arise for those playing client roles in remembering the factual details of their brief without inconsistencies or contradictions, but these are really unimportant and should not detract from the learning experience. It can be hard, too, though very valuable, to simulate responses of clients suffering from mental handicap, distress or confusion, factors which may all complicate the assessment process and which require extra care to ensure mutual comprehension, with the worker checking back even more conscientiously than usual that the communication has been clear and unequivocal. This can be quite extraordinarily difficult!

Bill, an elderly resident in a local authority home, exemplified several of these problems. He had a strong Devonshire accent, his speech was indistinct (he mumbled), he was of limited intelligence and did not relate well to other residents. No amount of practice with him, and no length of experience with other clients, could make workers sure that communication with him was really being effective; patience and the gradual learning of his idiosyncrasies were the only aids. On one occasion a worker was sitting with him, holding his hand and talking to him about quite a sensitive subject. From Bill's brief and mumbled responses it was unclear how much he had understood, but she noticed that his grip had tightened and his nails were digging into her hand. This was the only indication of his feelings; nothing could have been deduced from his facial expression.

Of course, if there is reason to think that a client's state of confusion or distress is likely to be transitory, it may be possible and desirable to defer some or all of the assessment process until she or he is calmer, but this is sometimes impossible, and indeed it may be the idea of the assessment itself which is agitating the client. If there is a need to prepare or rehearse the skills which are involved here (and it can be very useful), it will be found that emotional disturbance can be simulated in a role-play just as easily and convincingly as can mental handicap and deafness. There is a special need, however, to de-role afterwards, with participants talking briefly about their real selves in order to distance themselves from the emotions just enacted and reaffirm their own identity.

There is a certain paradox about assessment, in that while it is clearly something which arises out of our interaction with the client, we cannot necessarily make direct deductions from this interaction about how that client responds to people generally. Thus, when a client is being interviewed to assess her or his need for social skills training, she or he will quite possibly be able to respond and converse in an open, relaxed manner which in itself would give no hint of problems in social interaction; but here, of course, there is a worker who is taking all the initiatives, making every attempt to put the client at ease, in fact creating a quite abnormal social situation. This same client, relaxed and responsive in interview, may prove with other people, especially in a group, to be quite tongue-tied and inhibited. (This topic is explored in more detail in Chapter 3 on Assessment.) Hence it is useful to see clients in a group as well as a one-to-one situation, whether in a group of peers or of family members. It is, of course, very difficult both to be "in charge" of the interaction of the group and to try to reach some accurate conclusions about the behaviour of a member or members, and for this reason family therapists and group leaders working in pairs often differentiate their roles so that each of them is responsible for only one of the two functions.

RESPONDING TO NEEDS AND SHARING KNOWLEDGE; GIVING INFORMATION AND ADVICE; MAKING THINGS HAPPEN

In some ways it might seem natural to move directly from the subject of assessment to that of planning, but when, as here, the helping process is being considered in terms of interpersonal skills, such a transition may for various reasons not be appropriate. Other interactive skills may be brought into play before a joint plan can emerge, or there may be no need for a full plan to be agreed. Goldberg and Warburton (1979) noted in their study of the work of a Social Services department that 25% of cases were closed on the same day that they were opened and 64% within the first month. There may not be sufficient agreement between worker and client on overall aims and specific objectives for any real collaboration on a joint plan, and while this, of course, in no way precludes the need for a plan of work (indeed it could be seen as all the more necessary), it could not by definition involve any processes of interaction between worker and client. In such a case, however, there is an absolute obligation to keep clients informed of all developments which concern them, especially where actions of the worker's agency are concerned. Clients fiercely resent being kept in the dark about such developments, and with every justification, but the temptation to avoid or defer giving them this information can be a potent one.

Breaking unwelcome news is among the most unpopular social work tasks and examples will spring readily to mind, such as telling parents that their child has been removed, or is about to be removed, under a Child Protection Order, or that they have been refused the right to visit the child for the time being; telling a couple who have applied to foster or adopt that they are unsuitable; for a probation officer, telling a probationer who has reoffended that it is not possible to recommend that supervision should continue and what are the other, less desirable outcomes. The temptation to avoid or fudge such issues is enormous, and the situations involving the need to make unwelcome statements like these are among the ones most frequently cited by practitioners as causing them to feel anxious and unconfident. We have to try to find exactly the right words; whereas in other contexts it is the way in which the words are said, with accompanying non-verbal messages, which is often more significant than the words themselves, here the precise content of a statement is of such crucial importance that it makes sense to give a little time and thought to the actual choice of words. In a training situation, practitioners can often help each other by suggesting and discussing what needs to be said. How can you tell people about decisions which seem to condemn them as inadequate, uncaring, neglectful or cruel without seeming either to reject them as individuals unworthy of help or to dissociate yourself from the decision? It is hardest of all perhaps when the individual worker does not altogether support the policy of the agency, and hence has to communicate an unwelcome decision with which she or he is not in real agreement; or similarly when a probation officer, inwardly dissenting from the sentence of the court, has to discuss and explain it to the offender or his family.

On the whole, people who enter the helping professions like to see themselves as sympathetic and kindly, so they do not take readily to telling people things they do not want to hear, like the above unwelcome information; nor do they like refusing material aid or telling clients there is nothing they can do to help. Practice teachers sometimes remark that it is a new and unsought experience for students in placement to have to tell clients that no help is available or that what is being asked is not an appropriate thing for the worker to do—their first instinctive response is to comply if at all possible. It needs some reflection, and perhaps some practice as well, to be able to respond by a refusal, or an explanation of the limits within which the worker is operating.

Much short-term helping is, however, more like welfare rights and advice bureau work and other forms of social service, and has as its focus the more positive aspects of information-giving and explanation. Even when referring clients onward to another agency, it is often important to explain what they can expect from it, what its procedures are and particularly any disadvantages that may follow from contacting it. It is precisely when a worker is giving information on a very familiar subject that there is the greatest danger of leaving out some vital element or giving an unclear explanation, so care and attention can never safely be allowed to lapse, however thorough our own knowledge of the subject. In information and advice-giving, the factors mentioned above in relation to assessment as affecting a client's comprehension may assume even greater importance. Information and explanations will be given to a young child in quite different terms than to an adolescent, and allowance must obviously be made for the degree of mental handicap or emotional disturbance. Distressed or disturbed clients often have to be given some information several times over before they can really take it in. This is especially true of medical information, often given by doctors in terms that patients cannot understand and in a fashion which takes no account of their emotional state.

Where practical help is to be provided rather than simple information, the same degree of sensitivity to clients' emotional state and needs is called for if they are to be spared unnecessary distress.

> Marion, a very experienced and sensitive worker who was taking an old lady to a residential home, was careful to place herself between the woman and her family, so that they could not see her tears. All the family members, including the client herself, had agreed that the move was the right, indeed the only, course, but it was inevitable that she should feel a sense of loss and the family some guilt, and the worker was determined to minimize these feelings. Having eased the departure as far as possible, she held the old lady's arm supportively as they entered the home together and took time and care over the introductions to staff and residents (not too many at once!).

In circumstances like these, it is vital not to make a rushed departure to attend to other work, however pressing; a transition so momentous in its nature must not be hurried or disrupted.

Giving advice to clients is an activity traditionally frowned upon in the literature both on social work and on counselling, yet there is no activity which correlates more highly with the level of satisfaction clients express with the service given. What are we to make of this—simply that clients do not know what is good for them? This appears a rather presumptuous position. It seems more reasonable, and more humble, to argue that many helpers have been so anxious to avoid (quite rightly) selecting the aims which clients are to adopt that they have neglected to help in identifying and evaluating jointly with the client the steps by which those aims, once decided, can be achieved. This, then, is the essential criterion for advice-giving: that it should relate to the choice not of ends but of the means by which these ends are to be pursued, the choice of ends being a matter for selection by the client, or at least for mutual understanding between client and worker.

JOINT PLANNING

Some engagement and collaboration with the client is especially crucial for the planning stage in the helping process; many and varied research studies from that of Mayer and Timms (1970) onwards have demonstrated that agreement between client and worker on their choice of objectives is a major determinant of successful outcome and client satisfaction. This sounds very simple and obvious, so why, all too often, does it simply not happen? There are probably several reasons: a large volume of varied, demanding work can distract practitioners so that they are carried along by its momentum without taking the time to make a thorough assessment or re-evaluation and form a well-founded plan of intervention from it; they may have had a plan at the outset of their intervention but have to abandon it (without attempting to revise and modify it) in the face of sudden unforeseen developments; and finally, it is much easier for a worker to arrive at a plan of work in isolation divorced from the client. This last is the problem with which we are concerned here. It is a most powerful insidious temptation to devise a plan of action ideally suited to meeting the client's needs but without any real consultation and involvement—the client may be present, but without making any major contribution to the formulation of a plan of work and exercising very little influence over it.

With some kinds of statutory work it is obviously not possible for clients to have a deciding voice in planning, but in most instances they can and should be involved to the maximum. A useful model to apply here is that adopted by Reid and Epstein (1972), for whom the essence of planning lies in "shaping the task", a process in which the worker's function is defined as "to help the client shape the best possible course of action to remedy his difficulty". The criteria which should guide this selection are: the client's motivation; the feasibility of the task (can it be done?); and the desirability of the task (should it be done? is it appropriate to the problem?). To these criteria it would be useful to add credibility of the task for the client: not merely "can it be done?" but "does the client *believe* she or he can do it?".

In applying at least two of these criteria, the worker's interpersonal skills are of crucial importance; perception and sensitivity are required to reach a judgement about how much clients genuinely want to do something to resolve their problems and whether they really believe in their ability to do it. Neither of these factors is fixed, moreover. It is possible to increase the client's motivation and self-confidence, using some of the skills described in the previous chapter, but, conversely, these qualities may decline again when the client leaves the interview situation. Hence a great deal of skill and judgement is needed to arrive at joint decisions with clients about what they will have the ability, determination and confidence to attempt with a good chance of success. Reid and Epstein comment that "The practitioner's questions about feasibility serve to help the client shape or modify the task rather than to discourage him from pursuing it at all".

In such interchanges between client and worker there is often a transactional element of which it is important to be aware: the client may be able to unload so much of her or his own distress and anxiety onto the worker that the latter undertakes to carry out a variety of tasks that could equally well, and more appropriately, be carried out by the client. Offering or agreeing (sometimes as a result of pressure or manipulation) to take over from the client the main responsibility for working on her or his problems is unlikely to help in the long run, and may actually do harm. To be sure of avoiding this danger requires constant awareness of what is taking place in the interaction between worker and client as well as sensitivity to the client's needs and reactions. Clients who are good at making their workers feel guilty (like Phil's client described in Chapter 5) can often induce them to become involved in a lot of quite unnecessary activity on their behalf. Indeed, it is perhaps at the point where some plan of action needs to be formulated that workers are at their most vulnerable, after being bombarded by the client with a formidable array of needs and problems the weight of which now seems to be bearing down on them. Such a difficulty in disentangling oneself from this kind of confusion is familiar not only among students in training but also for experienced workers, as can be seen in case discussions held by support groups such as those run annually at Exeter University for local social workers and those described by Mattinson (1975). (See also Mattinson and Sinclair 1979.) Sharing one's own feelings about the case being worked with other practitioners can help one to recognize what is going on and give some clearer idea of the direction which future planning should take; role-play can then help further to make a shift in patterns of interaction that have effectively prevented any planning in the past. A good plan of action, in any context, is the product not of confused and inexplicit transactions but of genuine negotiation.

A lot of stress has been laid on the importance of the client's voice in planning, but the process can be enormously enhanced by the worker's ability to generate ideas, to be creative and encourage others to be so. One method of planning is to "brainstorm"—to produce ideas for possible solutions to a problem as rapidly as possible, simply listing them for possible discussion later without the slightest initial reflection on their feasibility (definitely *not* an approach to be recommended for *all* clients!). Suggestions can be "floated" successively by the worker in the most neutral possible way: this is an approach often required in divorce court welfare and conciliation work where, for instance, the custodial parent raises numerous objections to access to the children by the other parent. Essentially, the plan must be made by the separated couple themselves, but at least one of them, perhaps both, may have an interest in not resolving the problems over their arrangements and it requires someone outside the relationship to put forward some really positive proposals.

A decision on the course of action to be followed often brings with it a decision to involve others apart from the client and the immediate family: possibly other professionals, or perhaps the extended family, or friends and neighbours. Social workers in fact do spend a considerable proportion of their time in liaison of this kind with other agencies (Hallett and Stevenson 1980; Parsloe 1981) although it is possible that they do not exploit some resources, especially unofficial neighbourhood resources, as much as they might. In any case it is certain that this aspect of their work often requires interpersonal skills which are somewhat different from those which they are using with their client. In particular, a higher level of assertiveness is often needed and also, more specifically, the ability to formulate very clearly what the helper's role is in relation to the client in question and what help other professionals can usefully give. It can be very difficult to switch in a short space of time, as may be necessary, from a very gentle, sympathetic style of interaction (with a distressed client, for instance) to a firm, assertive approach with a doctor who is not taking his patient's problems seriously or a creditor who is trying to bully a client into giving his debt priority over all other expenditure. To be really effective, workers need to be versatile enough to move between these different styles of interaction, and it is particularly important that they should be able to articulate to other professionals the nature of the help they are planning to give clients without recourse either to vague, woolly generalizations or to stilted or pretentious use of jargon. This involves being clear in their own minds about what professional helpers can and cannot do; it also normally requires some experiment and practice with ways of formulating what they can offer.

CHAPTER 7 Skills demanded by particular contexts

The skills to be considered in this chapter are those interpersonal skills required specifically for working in contexts other than the one-to-one client and worker situation. Much of the classic casework literature (Hollis, for instance) is written as though this counselling situation constituted the entire material of social work activity and some practice training manuals give the same impression (eg Danbury 1979). Writers adopting a radical approach to practice have, however, focused attention on the need for workers to develop their ability to form and promote action systems which will operate to satisfy their clients' needs (eg Leonard 1975), and it is a powerful argument for an integrated approach to social work (as propounded by, for instance, Goldstein 1973; Pincus and Minahan 1973; Specht and Vickery 1977) that it requires any problems identified with clients to be considered, and if appropriate dealt with, in a group and community context as well as within the individual/family context. A constant complicating factor in the interpersonal skills which these varying situations demand is involvement with numbers of people rather than single individuals.

The classification of the skills for work with groups of people is a matter of even greater difficulty than the classification of counselling skills. Even systematic observation of group activities as rigorous as that undertaken by Rackham and his colleagues (1971) does not indicate any simple and reliable way of classifying group skills. Here, Colbert, Morris and Tribe (Rackham et al 1971) identified 27 behaviour categories fom videotaped recordings of group meetings, but these observations included unhelpful as well as productive behaviour, while shorter lists than theirs have always included residual "other behaviour" categories. The following list of behaviours which can properly be described as "skills" is drawn from the various observation and rating programmes of the Rackham group of trainers:

- Proposing
- Supporting
- Disagreeing and criticizing
- Building (rating a proposal and adding to it, making it more concrete)
- Clarifying
- Offering explanations, reasons and difficulties
- Seeking clarification, explanation, information
- Bringing in/shutting out
- Innovating
- Solidifying (consolidating or summarizing)
- Admitting difficulty
- Defending/attacking

It is interesting that the Rackham group were actually training senior airline staff in management skills, but they identified those skills as being essentially interpersonal ones, and specifically those required for working with groups of people.

The above list suggests at once why it is that interdisciplinary meetings—to which its relevance is immediately apparent—pose such a challenge to social workers, who do not often think of some of the behaviours listed there as part of their repertoire of professional skills. The idea of a professional helper criticizing, shutting out or attacking someone else clashes forcibly with the image of the caring, compassionate helper characterized by an accepting, non-judgemental attitude towards others. It might even appear at first sight that being a warm, gentle, empathic, caring professional was incompatible with being an effective committee member, and yet, in order to be fully effective, a caring professional needs interpersonal skills of both the empathic and the assertive type. While it is certainly arguable that nobody is perfectly qualified by nature to meet both kinds of demand and most people will lean towards one end of the spectrum or the other, nevertheless training and practice—with the usual proviso about accurate feedback—will usually permit the development of capacities which are latent but previously unused.

GROUP SKILLS

Under this heading it is proposed to consider skills specific to situations in which two or more clients are involved; it is important to remember that such skills are *additional* to the range of counselling and "process" skills described in the two previous chapters. It is for this reason, no doubt, that group and family work are experienced by practitioners as particularly demanding and tiring. In Perry's survey (1982), for instance, the probation officers consistently rated those interviews as "most professionally demanding" which involved interviewing two (or more) clients at once.

Awareness of the dynamics of a very complex piece of interaction and any necessary action to change those dynamics have to be balanced with response to the individual client's needs for empathy, reassurance and encouragement. At the same time, the worker may be trying to assess the clients or help them plan and select objectives. In a social skills training session, for instance, it is very likely that all these things will be going on simultaneously. What should be a realistic target for Pete to attempt? Will he have enough confidence to embark upon it in front of the others? Will Bob start to get impatient or disinterested if I neglect his problem while we work on this one? And whom can I enlist to help Pete work on his problem? Small wonder that one social worker described his social skills work as "perhaps the most demanding thing that I do".

Even if there is no specific involvement in groupwork as such, most professional helpers need to develop some group skills during their training. Home visits are as likely as not to involve several family members, and while this can in itself cause problems it can also shed light on the way members behave to each other. One of us remembers vividly visiting a woman client one morning during the school holidays when her son, aged 12 and deemed "maladjusted", was at home. She had previously talked to the boy at some length and been struck by how pleasant, friendly and articulate he was—the label "maladjusted" seemed something of a puzzle. Trying to talk to his mother in his presence was, however, another matter altogether; he displayed a range of infantile and disruptive behaviour which made it almost impossible to continue. Such incidents are familiar to many kinds of practitioner and recall Laing and Esterson's (1964) statement that anyone wanting to understand how a football team played together would go to see them play, not interview them separately; it is the more surprising that after Laing's initial diagnostic family interview he preferred to treat family members individually or in much smaller groupings (usually mother and daughter pairs), a practice which scarcely bears out the original analogy.

An interview with a family group in which the worker is not only observing and assessing the interaction but trying to help the family change this and experimenting with ways of doing so is, however, a very demanding and stressful one to conduct, and for this reason some form of joint working by two practitioners is usually recommended. Otherwise, one attention-seeking member like the boy described above can undermine any attempt to get things moving in a positive direction. In such joint work the practitioners often come from different professional disciplines, perhaps a social worker and a psychologist or a community psychiatric nurse.

In addition to the sheer complexity of the task of simultaneously observing what is going on between members and making a contribution to it, the practitioner is in danger of being drawn into the emotional interchange or conflict which is occurring. Two common forms which this danger can take are: the temptation to identify with one particular member of the family, perhaps because of some sense of sympathy or similarity; and manipulation by one family member into taking a certain stance, such as disciplining another member.

Handling such complex and subtle interchanges, then, involves a special range of skills, whether or not specific family therapy techniques are used. Whereas counsellors and psychotherapists in some settings (especially in private practice) can, if they wish, restrict their therapeutic activities to one-to-one interviews with clients, this is very seldom an option for workers in social services or multi-disciplinary community teams, even where there is no decision to undertake groupwork or to work with the family as a whole, and hence all basic training for the helping professions needs to give some attention to the development of these group skills. Indeed, specialized methods of working such as family therapy seem to require not additional or unusual skills, but simply a more conscious and structured use of skills needed in all aspects of their practice.

Sharing in a variety of (often commonplace) activities and experiences has always been a characteristic element in all forms of group care, whether in residential establishments or in day centres, and fieldworkers are increasingly recognizing the usefulness of involving themselves with their clients in day centres and various kinds of intermediate treatment and other activities projects as alternatives to care or custody. In this way, the artificial element which characterizes interviews with some clients can be avoided and the full potential for change exploited.

Bill, a children's houseparent, noticed that Tony, one of the boys in his unit, expressed contemptuous and disparaging attitudes towards girls and to female members of staff. An accomplished potholer, he took a group including Tony on a caving expedition, choosing an experienced young woman caver to accompany them so that Tony might in this way be put in the position of depending completely on a "strong" female —and also of offering her assistance in turn. This experience led, as Bill had hoped it would, to a general improvement in Tony's behaviour towards women and in his social relationships with them, an illustration of how changes in behaviour can *precede*, and indeed bring about, changes in attitude.

Types of Intervention

Of the skills involved specifically in group situations, the one which comes most readily to mind is that of controlling the group process, at least preventing it from taking certain forms and sometimes actually shaping it in a particular direction. A group leader is likely to have to intervene to ensure that the quieter or more timid members can participate adequately, or perhaps to prevent a more powerful member from assuming control, while in a family the habitual dominance of one member over another may need to be counteracted by the worker for any effective progress to be made.

This requires assertive skills in refusing to allow one member to take up all the discussion time, to answer for another or to put across his or her own views as if they were the only valid ones. Some such assertiveness may be called for in virtually all, even the least directive, groupwork situations, especially to protect the more vulnerable, and a family therapist will often help to foster positive interaction between members by saying in a very explicit and directive way, "Try this!" or "Talk to Jane for five minutes about what you like about her!" or "Say that directly to Pete, not just about him". Much the same style is called for in running social skills groups: "Try it again, and this time remember to look at him" or "Fine, we'll go on to your problem in a minute, but just now we're working on Barry's".

The controlling function of group leadership, however important, must not exclude the caring element, which, in addition to the same skills of empathy, support and encouragement required in individual work, involves fostering interchanges and alliances between the various clients present. They may need motivating to collaborate rather than to compete, and to help and support each other rather than mentally switch off when someone else is the focus of attention. Indeed, they may initially need help to feel comfortable in each other's company.

Combining these two kinds of skills, the controlling and the caring, when running a client group can be very demanding and where there are two leaders a useful device is to make a deliberate distinction in role between them, one being seen as the "task leader" and the other as the "social leader". Even if no such formal division is made, the participation of a second group leader means that it is always possible to compensate if one leader has been concentrating almost exclusively on providing control and direction, whereas for a worker trying to run a group alone it is really very difficult indeed to hold a balance between these two different functions.

A social skills group was working on a problem situation concerning Bob when a very garrulous member, Jim, in a way that was very typical of him, began contributing with the intention of being helpful but soon digressed into talking about his own situation. A leader said firmly, "Yes, but just now we're talking about Bob". At this, Jim subsided completely. The second leader noticed that he was uncharacteristically silent during the rest of the session and therefore made a point of talking to him briefly at the end, enabling Jim to say how badly he had felt about the episode and giving him some reassurance that he was really able to be a very caring and sympathetic member, even though he did need to work on giving more positive attention to others.

Other skills, relating to the fostering of group cohesion and mutual support, may involve interpreting one client's words or behaviour to another. If something one member has said gives unintended offence to another, or if it somehow misrepresents the real meaning of the speaker, the worker can often help by rephrasing this. A particularly useful family therapy technique called "reframing" involves taking up a topic which one family member has brought up as a complaint or source of resentment and looking at it in a positive rather than a negative light. Thus, if parents complain that their daughter is argumentative and spends too much time away from the home, this could be reframed by the worker in terms of the appropriately developing independence of an adolescent girl.

Such conflicts between family members also often require the worker to use negotiation and bargaining. Some family relationships make this extremely difficult to do: when, for instance, power is unequally shared between the two who are in dispute, as between a child and a domineering parent. The worker here has to try to find a way of supporting the weaker member without seeming to dispute the parent's authority and hence antagonize him (or her) further. An even more difficult and emotionally fraught type of negotiation is frequently encountered in divorce court welfare or conciliation interviews, in which resentment and bitterness are constantly surfacing and making it almost impossible for a separated couple to reach agreement on even the simplest practical arrangements for their children. There is probably no more tense and delicate situation which practitioners have to handle, and although newly qualified workers would not expect to take up this as a specialization, similar situations could be encountered at any time in more general practice, especially in view of the rapid expansion in the need for help of this kind.

Learning Groupwork Skills

Many of the group situations described above can offer opportunities for professional training and further development by means of associating an established worker with one who is less experienced or undergoing training, but this is not always possible and, even where it is, it may be useful to supplement the practice by the use of role-plays. Here again (as so often) it is particularly important to break off frequently, after perhaps as little as two or three minutes of interaction, to give participants a chance to discuss how best to proceed next. There is so much going on at the same time that those taking on the practitioner role feel swept along by the process.

Even quite experienced workers can benefit enormously from this kind of simulation when they are attempting a new method of work. In most, if not all, of the projects described in Section III of this book the practitioners, who were following an in-service training course, invited their fellow-students and the tutors to play the parts of a group of their clients, and this enabled them to become familiar and experiment with the new method before applying it *in vivo*. They reported that this was not only very convincing at the time but also very helpful when they came to try it out with their clients. Further help and support was provided by arranging for a tutor to join in one of the group sessions, thus permitting not only an assessment of the worker's skills but also encouragement and confirmation of the progress made. Students who are not in a position to set up a group of their own can sometimes be introduced into an existing client group, and we have described elsewhere (Collins 1981) an example of how students, after practice in a training group to familiarize them with the method, were introduced into specific sessions of a social skills group we were running at the same time for clients. This proved an extremely successful venture which was valued highly by clients and students alike.

SKILLS REQUIRED BY FORMAL SITUATIONS

When students and practitioners are asked what situations they find hardest to handle, always prominent among their responses are formal settings such as courts and multidisciplinary discussions and case conferences, together with public and other large meetings and hospital ward rounds. What such situations have in common is that they usually involve other professional workers, especially high-status professionals such as judges, lawyers, hospital consultants or other medical practitioners, and also individuals whose occupations give them other kinds of power, such as senior police officers or head teachers. Another common feature is that the actual setting (which is often the home ground of the other professional, such as court, police station or hospital) involves rules or expectations of which helpers such as social workers may be ill-informed or which conflict with their usual norms. There is often also the element of the worker being "in the firing line": that is, having to put forward an authoritative professional judgement and support it by argument and evidence, sometimes in the face of attempts to undermine or divert, or even naked bullying.

Of course, people widely perceived as powerful, who have an aura of authority and are used to getting their own way, are indeed inherently intimidating, and most people who do not share their advantages would find them so. Since the external trappings—the lawyers' wigs and gowns of a British court for instance—certainly make a contribution to this effect, some people find it helpful to imagine them without their finery or without their expensively tailored suits; in their gardening clothes, or even in their underwear.

But there is more to this difficulty than the powerful status and presentation of other professionals. In addition, there is a reluctance or an inability, especially among less experienced workers, to give a professional assessment or decision in a convincing and authoritative manner. All too often a social worker's opinion is given in a court or case conference in a manner which is diffident or, worse, woolly or imprecise, and in this way the stereotyped views which other professionals often hold about social workers as muddled or witless do-gooders are confirmed. To be effective, workers need to be able to state their professional opinion in such a way as to command respect. That much is obvious, but in order to do so they must believe that it does deserve that respect. The confidence in yourself that such a belief implies is not developed overnight. Rather, it is the task of professional training and supervision to foster its growth over a period of years. During the 1970s in Britain, many radical social workers expressed the view that they were not in fact professionals, had no special claim to knowledge or practice wisdom and were no different from their clients in any important respect (see, in particular, articles in *Case Con*, a radical social work journal published during this period). Whatever the positive contributions of this approach, its effect could only be to undermine the confidence we are discussing here, so it is particularly important that, both during and after training, practitioners have the opportunity to discuss issues of this kind and to work out for themselves the basis of their professional approach and authority.

Once the underlying uncertainties and insecurities have been resolved, the way is open to develop skills of professional presentation by rehearsal, with progressive shaping, prompting and encouragement where appropriate, and it is probably in this context that training in professional interpersonal skills gives the best results in terms of both improvement in performance and increased confidence for practitioners. Encouragement and reinforcement are particularly important, and it is all too easy for the others present at a role-play to rush in immediately with criticisms such as: "I couldn't hear you!", "You let him shift you from your original point of view", or "Why didn't you stand up straighter?". Such comments may be very much to the point, and slightly later they will be helpful, indeed essential, but—just like the client in a social skills group—the first thing the practitioner needs after attempting something particularly difficult is some sign of acceptance, an explicit reassurance that at least something has been done right, that the basic elements are there out of which a truly skilled performance may develop.

At this stage, too, useful practical tips may be offered. For instance, an individual standing while the (more powerful) other or others are seated is usually at a disadvantage and may feel and look awkward; taking a seat may help in itself. For anyone who has to remain standing, an asymmetric stance with one foot slightly in front of the other and one hand on a doorway or a desk-top usually both feels more comfortable and looks more relaxed, as self-observation on video will confirm. Not knowing what to do with your hands when the spotlight is on you is a common experience, and holding even so small an object as a pen can feel surprisingly reassuring and has the added advantage of discouraging irritating mannerisms like scratching a beard or other hand-to-face movements, which tend to detract from effective communication.

Types of Intervention

The actual content of intervention is often similar to that described above as required in group situations of a more general kind, but a more formal and incisive *style* of intervention is often required. Group members are more likely to appear powerful and authoritative (perhaps even intimidating) and practitioners may have to confront and correct misperceptions of their role and the powers and limitations of their agency. Hallett and Stevenson (1980) stress that "whenever individual workers collaborate, they bring both their own professional identity and their views about the role, status and frames of reference of other professionals". After referring to the difficulty which this process involves in relation to child abuse procedures, however, they go on to note that social work students have been found to rate "attending meetings" and "committee behaviour" as among the least important elements of their training. Their study of case conferences in fact shows that some aspects of communication which might in other contexts seem fairly straightforward produce a surprising degree of difficulty in this interdisciplinary setting: for instance, there was a reluctance to ask for clarification of terms used by other professionals when these were not understood. Social workers also tended to use terms of their own without sufficient explanation to other professionals, especially legal terms such as Place of Safety Order (now superseded by Child Protection Order), the implications of which were often not understood by others.

The practitioner who is actually chairing such a meeting or case conference is clearly in a demanding situation, having to display many of the ordinary groupwork skills such as keeping members to the task and ensuring that all have the opportunity to contribute when there may well be one or two powerful people present who are themselves more familiar with the leadership role and may even mount a bid to assume control of the current group. While the more taxing and momentous type of meeting, such as child protection conferences or reviews, would normally be chaired by a worker of senior status, there are many other interdisciplinary meetings in the context of community care which may be convened and chaired by any worker from the range of helping professionals involved. This activity is likely to increase in scope and importance as we try to improve the quality of care available to people in their own homes. The person chairing such a group is likely to have to exercise all the skills demanded of someone running a client group, possibly with a higher level of assertiveness on occasion and in combination with other, additional skills.

Irrespective of who is in charge of the proceedings, the various professional helpers present will usually be expected to deliver a clear, articulate and authoritative account of matters within their knowledge and competence, such as a succinct account for the benefit of a court or case conference of work undertaken with individual clients or families or of the functions, powers or resources of their agencies. The ability to talk to an informal or semiformal gathering of doctors and nursing staff about what service medical social workers can provide and what problems are appropriately referred to them is often a prerequisite to the provision of an effective service for the wards concerned.

The unfamiliar setting and strange roles of other participants, together with the authority (or perhaps the pretentiousness) of some of the figures present, all combine to make it difficult for the worker to come across as clear, authoritative and knowledgeable, and to do so without the use of professional jargon, something which most workers maintain they abhor but which tends to slip out under pressure. Situations like these, more than any others perhaps, lend themselves to rehearsal in group sessions with particularly valuable results, and we ourselves have been convinced how useful this can be by the enthusiastic way in which practitioners who have trained with us still talk several years later about this vivid and memorable learning experience. In the scenario about which the greatest anxieties are expressed, that of the social worker responding to questioning in court, some very simple suggestions can helpfully be borne in mind (and it is vital that they be kept simple, since high levels of anxiety would otherwise obliterate them). Such suggestions will include adopting a posture which is both comfortable and alert, taking time to answer in a reflective, unhurried manner, and maintaining eye contact with the magistrates or judge rather than with the (potentially hostile) lawyer who is putting the questions. In addition to rehearsing these techniques it is also a wise measure to prepare carefully in advance for each specific occasion of this type. Since you will know that you are likely to be questioned on certain points, or that you are going to be presenting a particularly delicate piece of work at a case review meeting, it is both practicable and sensible to hold your own mental review of the case you are making before the actual occasion presents itself. In this way it is possible to identify any points which you may need to clarify further or on which you might need to marshal additional evidence or arguments.

COMMUNITY WORK SKILLS

It is noteworthy that whereas many helpers will work both on an individual and group basis with clients, community work is more often seen as a distinct activity, with a separate corps of practitioners.

Table 7.1. Process and tasks in community organization

Stages of process	Worker tasks	
	Technical tasks	Interactional tasks
Socialization groups: socialization	Identify and define problems	Identify potential members; motivate and recruit members; educate constituency
Primary groups: develop affective relations	Link problem identification to goal development	Cultivate social bonds and build group cohesion
Organization–development groups: build organizations	Develop programme objectives and organization structures	Broaden constituency; build a coalition; develop leadership
Institutional relations organizations: mediate the relations between individuals and institutions	Implement strategy (administration and planning)	Participate in organizational enrichment and change through use of tactics: education, persuasion, bargaining and pressure

Source: Brager and Specht (1973). Reproduced by permission of the authors and Columbia University Press.

Nevertheless, a certain evolution in attitudes can be discerned in Britain, where, during the nineteen sixties, it was seen as sufficiently distinct for a study group to be set up to consider the nature of its activity and make recommendations about training (Calouste Gulbenkian Foundation 1968). Fourteen years later, the Barclay Report (Barclay Committee 1982), while still identifying community workers as a distinct group and noting that the evidence they received "indicated that few identify themselves as social workers", went on to describe social workers as carrying out "activities overlapping, but not coextensive with those of community workers" (para. 10.21), and then to develop a community-oriented approach to social work which requires skills of advocacy, negotiation and bargaining, working with community networks and setting up and developing projects, in addition to the more traditional helping skills. Many of the skills used in the practice of community work, however, are identical, or at least very similar, to those used in other forms of helping. This point is well illustrated by the model put forward by Brager and Specht (1973) (Table 7.1).

The technical tasks listed in the second column of Table 7.1 are already familiar to us; they correspond closely to some of the inter-personal skills discussed in Chapters 5 and 6 as involved in the practice of social work and other forms of helping activity. The second group of worker tasks, shown in the third column and described as "interactional", are similar to the groupwork skills described earlier in this chapter, particularly activities such as motivating members, cultivating social bonds and building group cohesion. Some activities under the "worker tasks" heading appear, however, to go beyond what ordinary groupwork would require. Activities which are usually seen as more specific to community work would include identifying and recruiting suitable members (and, it is important to add, discouraging unsuitable members) and bringing about organizational change through tactics which include persuasion, bargaining and pressure.

This last group of skills obviously involves the greatest degree of assertiveness, of toughness and "push" of any described here, exem-plifying an approach somewhat alien to the notion of community work as an essentially non-directive activity (Batten 1967), which seems to comprise simply "stimulating people" by questioning what they may want to do and how they might achieve it, a "soft" activity similar in character to some counselling approaches which exclude the elements of challenge and confrontation. How would such a truly non-directive community worker act when trying to help a tenants' association to achieve their goals if these included trying to expel members of a minority ethnic group or concentrate them in the most run-down block on the estate? To be honest and effective, a worker must be able to challenge the appropriateness of community members' goals and the methods by which they plan to achieve them wherever this is needed. The interpersonal skill which this requires is essentially that same skill of challenge which was discussed in Chapter 5 in relation to work with individual clients but it can, of course, be more difficult to practise it in the community context, where the worker may feel under a great deal of pressure from one or two quite emphatic or domineering individuals. Even more intimidating would be a setting in which the consensus among those with whom the worker was trying to operate was in such clear conflict with the worker's values that the only remaining option was dissent and withdrawal. But, always, the decision when to express such difference, challenge or dissent is particularly difficult in the community context because it always has to be made with due consideration for the other issues obtaining at the time.

A further requirement of the neighbourhood worker as distinct from other professional helpers is a good knowledge and understanding of local administrative and political structures and of the way power is distributed and exercised at local level. Such knowledge can then decide what skills it is appropriate to employ, and with whom. It is no use trying to motivate an official to carry out an action which is beyond his power, however persuasively the case for that action may be argued. Moreover, knowledge about the powers (and some of the personal qualities) of officials and other individuals with whom it will be necessary to negotiate will be needed to enable the community worker to decide who would be the best person to undertake the negotiation—whether the actual worker or a member of the community, and if the latter, then which member.

The same kind of ability to select and encourage people to take part in activities according to their individual potential is involved in working with volunteers. When a community project is being set up with the participation of volunteers, difficult decisions sometimes have to be made about those who are unsuitable for the tasks which will need to be done—perhaps they are set on "helping" in inappropriate ways or are unaware of the upsetting effect they may have on vulnerable poeople. The worker then has to persuade them to alter their own approach: either to help in a different role to which they may be better suited or, in some cases, to withdraw altogether—and all this as tactfully as may be, with the least possible loss of face and self-esteem in the would-be volunteer.

Since community work is often seen as distinct from social work, there exist specific training courses for community workers, but there are also social work courses with an option in community work. It is, moreover, possible to find workers in generic or other area social work teams or in multidisciplinary specialist teams who carry out some of the activities typically associated with neighbourhood work, such as setting up a day centre, drop-in centre or other community project. Many of such workers will have had little or no training specifically preparing them for community work, yet they find themselves doing it. It therefore seems important that courses which train generic social workers, and perhaps other helpers too, should identify and address the areas of skill needed in community work, and in particular give more attention to work with volunteers: people, that is, who, like foster parents or helpers in a day centre, are not clients and not exactly professional colleagues. On courses which do not specifically offer a community work specialism, it is fairly unusual for students to have opportunities in placement to develop such skills. However, this is an area in which classroom simulations and role-plays are particularly useful, providing the emphasis is not on what this alien breed of community worker does but on what you yourself may want to know and how you might operate as a flexible worker wishing to be involved in community activities.

Moving from the development of skills of empathy and reflection to those which are in question here involves a considerable discontinuity, and some of the group skills cited at the beginning of this chapter such as disagreeing and criticizing, shutting out, defending and attacking may seem really alien to many students, arousing considerable anxiety and discomfort. Some, especially those with the most explicit commitment to sharing and empathy with individual clients, may not even feel sure that they want to develop in this direction at all. The experience of training needs to include ample opportunity for all to examine and discuss issues of this kind which bear so closely upon the nature of the professions on which they are embarking. Indeed, the whole process of training for the helping professions within the college setting can offer excellent opportunities both to explore one's own ethical and ideological position and to develop skills of this kind. Lively debate with other students and the onus of presenting reasoned and well-supported arguments and defending them against attack by other course members are not expensive luxuries added to professional training programmes by empire-building academics; they are experiences of direct relevance and value to subsequent professional practice.

Case illustrations

Three brief case illustrations will help to demonstrate some of the special skills involved in work in the community context. These short accounts exemplify the lack of structure and clarity with which community workers often have to grapple, their difficulty in finding a useful and acceptable role for themselves and the lack of consensus, indeed the occasional conflict of interests, between those they are trying to help.

The first concerns Paul, a student placed in a family centre run by a voluntary organization who had great difficulty in finding a role for himself alongside the experienced established worker, who was strongly identified with the community in which the centre had been set up. He listened attentively to the concerns and needs expressed by the women attending the centre and found that they consistently complained about difficulties in shopping, and specifically about the shortcomings of local facilities. After some reflection, he therefore suggested to them that it might be possible to hire a minibus and make a joint excursion to a nearby city with an excellent shopping centre, a suggestion which was immediately welcomed by the group of women with a great deal of enthusiasm. Thus encouraged, Paul proceeded to make some further enquiries about the detail of how to organize such an excursion and brought his findings back to the group, only to find that their initial enthusiasm had evaporated and that no-one was willing to make any personal commitment to it. He later found that this episode exemplified the difficulties of helping the group to change anything in their situation; they would repeatedly complain about various aspects of it, but would not commit themselves to anything which might achieve any improvement, consistently allocating all responsibility and power to things outside themselves. This is a pattern of response which would almost certainly call for some kind of challenge from the worker if the context were that of individual counselling, but in that of community work the undertaking is much more complex and difficult.

The second case, described by Holmes and Bryant (1977) in a chapter about fieldwork teaching in community work, also illustrates the unpredictable and often disappointing elements in community work. The student was assigned to work with a newly formed group in an inner-city area in Glasgow, but found that it was starting to disintegrate; two days before a meeting which he was helping to organize the chairman and committee all resigned. The meeting, which was concerned with the authorities' plans to develop the neighbourhood, was in fact attended by an audience of some 400 local people, who asked many questions of the officials who addressed them, but despite this only about a dozen people left their names in response to a handout. Disappointingly small though this group was, it was sufficient to form the nucleus of a new committee convened by the student, leading to the emergence of a viable residents' association. It is clear how important a part was played in this by the student's perseverance in distributing leaflets about the meeting himself, in the absence of any committee members to help, finding a new chairman and recruiting the nucleus of a new organization.

Thirdly, Jordan (1973), writing about his work with claimants' unions in Devon, describes the formation of a new group formed out of ". . . an alliance between two groups who had previously been mutually suspicious or even hostile . . . united in their hatred of the Social Security". These were, on the one hand, well-established residents from the town's council estates comprising redundant local workers, pensioners and single parents, and, on the other, mostly single migrant workers from other parts of the country, who lived in flatlets and bed-sitting-rooms in the town centre. Such a mix did not make for instant harmony, and early meetings were described as "overcrowded, noisy, chaotic, disorderly, quarrelsome and very exhausting". Despite these features and the clashes in perspective of the two groups of members, the branch did eventually achieve cohesion, stability and a democratic structure, but along the road it had to resolve the difficulties generated by such authoritarian tendencies as moves to "make its organisation hierarchical and exclusive, to fine non-attenders, to exclude certain individuals, to exclude women, and to concentrate authority in a few hands". Any developments of this type will inevitably pose problems for a community worker in terms of how to oppose them without seeming actually to impose his or her own ethos on the group.

These three examples illustrate both the unpredictable and sometimes chaotic scene in which community work often takes place and the need for anyone working in this context to command a wide range of assertive skills and to be clear about the ideological issues on which a stand needs to be taken.

SECTION III

Skills training with client groups and how it may be practised

This section moves on to describe social skills training with a variety of different client groups. It demonstrates, mainly through the medium of case studies, how different kinds of group may be set up and the special considerations which may apply with particular clients or in particular group care settings. These case studies are intended not as a statistical evaluation of the method but as examples of good, imaginative practice which may serve to stimulate and encourage others.

CHAPTER 8   Social skills training with groups in the community

The third section of this book is concerned with the use of skills training methods to help clients develop new ways of tackling situations that pose problems for them and generally to improve the quality of their interaction with others. Workers in residential and daycare settings are, typically, concerned with specific client groups, and we shall be going on to discuss the special considerations involved and to give case illustrations relating to a number of such groups, but in the present chapter we shall be discussing social skills groups in more general terms, thinking particularly of the kind of mixed groups which might be run by workers in a community team. There is a simple logic in starting in this way when describing the method of work, but it is an inevitable temptation for practitioners who are starting to learn the method for use with a particular client group to exclaim "But that wouldn't work with my clients! They'd never be able to do that".

In particular, practitioners often express doubts as to whether clients will actually volunteer tangible problems which can be worked on, expecting a response in terms either of all the faults lying in past and present circumstances or in other people, or of emotional conflict or deprivation, so that when they come to invite clients to contribute ideas about problem areas they are quite surprised to find how readily many of them respond.

Why Provide Social Skills Training in a Group?

The methods described here can usually be employed with equal effectiveness in individual work with a single client, but for several reasons it is frequently most convenient to use the approach with a group of clients. First, sharing of problems helps the members to realize that they are not unique in the problems they experience.

They can contribute suggestions as to how the problems experienced by others can be tackled (and perhaps gain confidence from the fact that they can cope with situations others find difficult). Indeed, such a suggestion by a member can be more appropriate, on occasion, than something offered by the group leader, who might be different in age and gender. Adolescents, for instance, can often model for each other much more effectively than an older person can model for them. Lastly, the situations that make clients most anxious often involve a number of people, so that a group is the natural forum for working on them.

Distinguishing Features of Social Skills Groups

It seems necessary at this stage to define the kind of group with which we are concerned because of the increasingly widespread use of the term "social skills" to refer to activities which in fact have no *social* component whatever, merely involving self-care (such as eating and dressing) or knowledge of procedures such as obtaining welfare benefits. Moreover, many so-called "social skills groups" do not in fact use any particular method and are simple discussion groups about the social problems of members. The following are essential features of social skills groups as we understand and use the term:

1. They require members to identify specific, concrete interpersonal situations which cause them concern;
2. They involve behavioural rehearsal of these situations, not simple discussion;
3. They aim to produce a change in the way participants behave, or at least in the way they *can* behave.

A group from which one of these elements was missing might well be experienced as helpful, but it would not be a social skills group.

There is a very wide range of purposes which social skills training may serve. One related form is assertiveness training (cf Phelps and Austin 1975), which has been extensively used, especially by women's groups in the USA and more recently in Britain too. Such an approach rests on the assumption that women tend to learn various inappropriate or ineffective forms of behaviour as part of their socialization process, such as passive or manipulative types of response. Hence, they may benefit from being helped to develop a non-aggressive, assertive behavioural repertoire. Timid teenagers wanting to improve their ability to make friends just before or just after leaving home, withdrawn or agoraphobic housewives (of any age), youngsters (especially, but not exclusively, boys) who easily get into an aggressive confrontation with peers or adults, could all be helped by social skills training. Apart from the obvious and frequently encountered job interviews, the situations identified and worked on could include interchanges with other family members (parents, children, spouses, siblings) or with landladies, social security officials, professionals of various kinds, peers, older people, the opposite sex—the list is virtually endless. The golden rule is that the situations are those that the clients want to work on.

The question might be asked, whether the members of such a group might have aims for themselves which the leaders—or other group members—find unacceptable. In theory, such goals might be to develop the ability to manipulate or persuade others so as to obtain an unfair advantage over them. Indeed, methods such as the present ones may be used in the training of sales representatives (insurance salesmen, for instance), and feminists have been known to refuse to participate in any process which could be seen as teaching young men to make sexual advances. Such anxieties seem disproportionate to the potential gains to be made by the inhibited, timid youngsters with whom we have worked, but there might occasionally be instances where the workers would want to question: "Do we really think that's something we should be helping you to try to do?".

In practice most social skills groups seem to be predominantly male in composition, and if there is a "typical" group member he is probably in his late teens or early twenties and could well be rather below average in intelligence (although we have had professional and mildly mentally handicapped members in the same group, with surprisingly positive results). In theory, however, there is no reason to think any particular age group more likely to benefit, and we have been particularly struck by the fact that students who are learning to use the method frequently suggest a socially isolated woman, often an older woman and perhaps an agoraphobic, when asked to present a client for whom the approach might be helpful;

subsequent role-plays, with the students playing the client, will suggest they are right. It seems as if the referring agencies (often in the psychiatric field) have a stereotype of the social skills client as a young male and thus it does not occur to them to refer an older female.

There are, of course, problems inherent in having a group whose members show a wide disparity of age, intelligence and background, but there are also advantages, and provided that sufficient goodwill is present they can actually give each other a great deal of help. A group in which all members experience identical problems, and to a similar degree, can place tremendous strain on the leaders. Clients who, while they do have problems of their own, experience no great difficulty with the situation with which other group members are struggling can contribute a great deal of help; it can also enhance their image of themselves to be seen, and to see themselves, in a helping role. The one kind of client who cannot be safely included in such a group is the man (or woman) who is so heavily defended that she or he cannot disclose her or his own problems and responds to other members with biting, critical or sarcastic comments.

Method of Working

Group leaders need to talk to members of the future group in advance. This is necessary not only for purposes of selection—that is, to determine whether the clients are suitable for this method of help, and how they are likely to fit in with other prospective members—but also to enable them to understand what they are committing themselves to in joining such a group and what the experience will be like. Because the method and style of such groups (though not the content) is predetermined, it certainly cannot be said that "you can make of it what you want", so genuine commitment from members is essential. They have to recognize that they will be looking at the way they behave and trying out ways of changing it, so it is certainly not a group for people who only want to dwell on past misfortunes, explore their present emotional state or locate the responsibility for anything that is going wrong in their lives entirely with other people. Clients sometimes present themselves for social skills training because someone—usually a psychiatrist—has told them that this is something that they need, but without any real conviction that they would benefit from changing any aspect of their behaviour. They are, therefore, quite likely to drop out of a social skills group at an early stage, so it is really preferable if one of the leaders can recognize their low motivation at the selection stage and advise against joining so as to start with a group comprising only well-motivated clients.

A group of this particular kind, more perhaps than any other, really requires *two* leaders, and indeed it may well benefit from the presence of a third. (Chapters 3 and 6 both highlight the advantages of dividing group leadership functions between two workers.) This is because leaders are frequently called on to participate as well as to direct. The style of leadership required, too, is a very directive one: group members need to feel that the leaders are *in control* of what happens, so that it is safe to bring up, and enact, some situations which provoke in them very high levels of anxiety. Control is also required to ensure that the group's time is appropriately and fairly shared between members.

Structuring the sequence of sessions, and of role-plays within individual sessions, requires a careful build-up from the least threatening topics to the more difficult. Early role-plays are often chosen to be applicable to everyone, not specific to individual members, so that all can recognize what kind of difficulties are involved and what approach is to be used. Examples could be stock situations like protesting when a stranger pushes in front of others in a bus queue, or returning faulty goods to a shop. These get things moving in the group without asking members to reveal their own weaknesses before they are ready to do so. Once work begins about individual problems, the leaders have to be careful to ensure a gradual progression from the simplest, least threatening form of the situation to something which approximates to the level of difficulty which members are likely to encounter. If the task in hand is maintaining her or his position against an unreasonable neighbour or relative, the client is likely to protest, after the first attempt at a run-through: "Oh, he wouldn't give in as easily as that" or "No, he's much more irritable than John was". The level of such difficulties can be stepped up progressively as the role-play is rerun and clients can tackle these with increasing confidence because of the success achieved in the easier versions, but clients must never be set up to fail. They have, for the most part, already had too much experience of failure. The leaders always have a nice calculation to make before embarking on a role-play: is the member ready to do this role-play now, in this form?.

Before role-plays of any personal situations begin, a number of facts need to be established. Who else was involved? What were they like? Were they sitting or standing up? Where in relation to you? What exactly was said, by whom, and in what kind of voice? What happened then? What did it feel like? It is a point worth noting that while the feelings experienced are relevant, indeed important, they should merely be recognized, not dwelt upon at any length, since this causes the group to lose momentum and discussion can become bogged down (playing the game of "Ain't it awful!"). One of the most difficult operations involved in working on members' interpersonal problems is devising situations which encapsulate these problems in terms specific enough to allow work to be done on them. Patience and imagination, with the capacity for eliciting factual details from the member in question, are what is needed at this stage, but once a situation has been identified going on to role-play it as soon as possible helps to prevent a build-up of anxiety.

Sometimes the best—even the only—way to show what the situation was like is to role-play it as it actually happened, rather than with the member concerned making a conscious effort to improve his performance. In this case, it is particularly important, but also often very difficult, to give this initial role-play a warm and sympathetic reception. This group member has just depicted an exchange in which he felt a total failure and the last thing he needs from the group is confirmation of how badly he did it. What he does need is to be thanked and praised for his honesty, and where there are objective difficulties in the situation (ie things most people would find it difficult to cope with) it often helps to identify them. Also needed is some explicit reassurance that the group will indeed help with his problem situation.

A situation like opening a conversation with a strange girl or a girl known only by sight is usually seen as very threatening by most (male) group members, but it is usually possible to work up gradually towards such an undertaking. In our groups, we have started this process by one of the leaders taking a direct part in the early role-plays, since an older woman who has already shown the will and the ability to help members with their problems (and no disposition whatever to criticize or mock them) is usually the *least* threatening kind of female figure to act as partner. The next stage has been to introduce social work students into the group, one or two at a time, to participate in the role-plays. These women are necessarily more of a threat in that they are younger, often about the members' own age, and not previously known to them. On the other hand, their sympathy can be assumed, and they are particularly adept at "grading" their responses so as not to intimidate the more anxious members and giving progressively less help and encouragement (*during* role-plays that is—not afterwards) as participants become increasingly skilled in approaching them.

The inevitable question remains, however: even when skills have been learned and practised in the (relatively) secure atmosphere of group meetings, can they really be reproduced in real-life situations? This question of generalization is a crucial one, and certainly the evidence of improved performance in the practice situation is much more conclusive than is evidence of generalization of such skills outside that situation. This is not to say, of course, that such improvement does not take place; it may simply be that evidence for it is harder to collect. If it is asked whether the girl-shy, awkward, tongue-tied adolescent boy can actually start to make friendships with the opposite sex following a series of practice sessions such as we have described, it does sound rather unlikely. But we can remember vividly Tony, a member of one of our groups, who was so terrified of opening a conversation with a girl that he shook all over while completing a short role-play (after a similar scene had been enacted by other members) in which he walked into an office adjacent to the one where he worked and addressed a simple request to the typist there (role-played by a social work student). One of the leaders had to stand close by him throughout the short scene, and could feel him trembling, then accompanied him out of the room to give him a (short) chance to express his intense feelings of anxiety but also to praise him emphatically for not allowing them to stop him from completing the scene. He was certainly one of the most inhibited members of the group and the progress he made was slow, but a year or two after the sequence finished one of the leaders met Tony by chance in the street and was pleased (though somewhat surprised) to learn that Tony was now leading a much more active social life (previously he had stayed at home with his family and watched TV) and actually had a girl friend!

Sometimes, the generalization of the behaviour learned can be helped by encouraging group members to take on activities together, in pairs or in groups. A woman who is somewhat agoraphobic, for instance, might be more willing to undertake an excursion to the city centre if it has been agreed that she will meet another member there for shopping or to have a cup of tea. A group of young men from one group arranged to meet at a bar known locally for its music and spent two or three hours there; when asked afterwards how long it was since they had done anything similar, several replied that they had *never* before made a similar excursion. "Homework" tasks like this are very effective in helping to generalize the behaviour which has been learned in group sessions.

A last feature of crucial importance for this method of working is reinforcement. It is impossible to overemphasize the need to reinforce every attempt by a client and every improvement in performance over the previous version. Even when there has been no clear improvement, it is still possible to say something like: "OK Pete, thanks for doing it again. Your voice was still nice and clear —just about right for loudness—but, if you remember, you were going to try to look at him while you were speaking to him. Could you just try it again, and this time remember to keep looking at him while you're speaking". Perhaps some visual cues or prompts might be added next time, since the client is obviously finding this difficult, and if he has not succeeded it is appropriate that the leaders should take some responsibility for this. "Perhaps I didn't give you enough help" or "Perhaps I didn't make my suggestions clear enough" or "Perhaps we could try a simpler version" are all appropriate and relevant comments in such a situation, since it is the leaders' responsibility to try to identify tasks at which clients can succeed. Clients who have plenty of experiences of failure behind them certainly do not need us as their helpers to provide them with any more. It is for this reason, too, that their need for consistent reinforcement and reassurance is so great.

Not all the reinforcement is provided by the leaders, however. Early on in the life of a group, members can be encouraged to follow the examples of the leaders and offer support, praise and encouragement as well as any hints they may want to volunteer about changes and improvements. Some clients find this difficult and need quite a lot of prompting, while any members who seem likely to jump in with undermining or destructive comments have to be handled particularly tactfully.

A Case Illustration

There is no better way to demonstrate the way a social skills group operates than by giving a detailed description of one or two sessions, a kind of group process recording. In order to illustrate how the method can help people with a variety of problems, two sessions will be described from our work with social skills groups in the community. Some details have been changed to protect members' anonymity, but the individuals, together with their problems and the work they did on them, are real. Thumbnail sketches of the six people to be included, together with the purpose of their involvement in a social skills group, are all that is required for an understanding of the work they did with us.

Ronnie, in his middle thirties, had spent a number of years in psychiatric units for violent offenders, but was at this point living in lodgings. He was generally amiable and compliant in manner but given to violent outbursts on occasion, and moreover felt socially isolated because of his long period in hospital.

Neil, a young man about 30, still living with his parents and brother, was referred by a clinical psychologist whom he had been seeing for a drink problem, in which his high social anxiety seemed to play a part. He expressed a wish to improve his skills in meeting and mixing with people and in interaction with others he knew already (family, people at work).

Toni, a young housewife in her mid-twenties, had spent a period in a psychiatric hospital some time before joining a previous group. We have described elsewhere (Collins and Collins 1981) the work she did on two very specific situations, but she also suffered from more generalized anxiety about meeting people and in fact had in the past been labelled agoraphobic.

Fran was 17, a student following a secretarial course at the local college. She was referred by the college counsellor as being very timid in group situations, anxious about getting to know new people and finding it difficult to stand up for herself.

Pete was in his late twenties, of very limited intelligence, indeed on the borderline of mental handicap. Unlike most of this group (who were in general rather small and timid in appearance), Pete was well-built and had a fairly confident, cheerful expression and an infectious laugh; this last is a subject to which we shall return.

Jim, also in his late twenties, was in other ways a complete contrast to Pete (in fact these two members of the same group were able to offer each other considerable mutual help and support). He was a graduate who had spent a few weeks in psychiatric hospital the previous year following a breakdown, since when he had gained help from a therapeutic group but needed to do some more work building up his confidence in various social situations, particularly job interviews.

The leaders were John and Mary (the present authors) and Paul, a friend who was a clinical psychologist. We always enjoyed working together and our different personalities and backgrounds complemented each other well, Paul being initially the best versed in the technicalities of the method, John being the most outgoing in manner and Mary being probably the most supportive and gentle with the more timid members, especially the women.

The work to be described would be appropriate to about the third or fourth sessions in a sequence of 8 to 10 weekly meetings. The first session is usually kept very short and consists mainly of getting to know each other, possibly over a cup of coffee, and an explanation of the methods which will be used. The second session probably begins with a brief recapitulation of that explanation (since it is likely most members may be sufficiently anxious to require a repetition for them really to take it in). Typically, it continues with some very simple, commonplace situations which have no particular personal applications, such as protesting when a stranger queue-jumps in the post office or at the bus stop, or initiating a conversation with someone known by sight—something which does not ask participants to reveal anything about themselves and is not too threatening and risky for the more timid members. It concludes with agreement on homework, which at this early stage will probably not be dependent on individual situations but the same for everyone: let us say, for example, that each member will initiate a short conversation with someone he or she meets casually, in a shop or a bus queue perhaps.

The third session begins as usual with the leaders asking members in turn how things have gone for them in the week since the last meeting and in particular about their "homework" assignment. Ronnie describes a quite short but pleasant chat he had with someone he met waiting in the post office; things generally have been "not too bad" but he is frustrated becase he cannot get any satisfaction at the radio shop to which he took his transistor about six weeks ago. The proprietor originally told him it would be ready in about 10 days, but Ronnie has now called back several times only to be told that he is "waiting for a part". He is getting very frustrated about this, though apparently he replied (even on this last occasion) "Oh, all right, then". A leader comments that this may be something we could usefully come back to and turns to Toni, who says she has had a quiet week, with no particular problems, and has managed to start a brief conversation with another mother whom she sees at the nursery group to which they both take their children.

Neil, who speaks next, has also initiated a conversation with someone he knows only by sight. No difficulties there, but he has had problems at work with the foreman, who, he feels, is always "having a go" at him, niggling and criticizing at every opportunity. Yes, Paul (a leader) agrees, that makes for a pretty uncomfortable work situation. What sort of things do you say to him? Do you find that you're niggling and sniping at him a lot of the time too? Neil agrees that's probably so, and we start to explore whether he can think of some more positive kinds of exchange he might initiate with the foreman—another possible situation to drop back to later in the meeting.

Fran, next, tells us that "nothing special has happened" to her in the past week. At first she doesn't think she has *started* a conversation with anyone, but then remembers she spoke to a girl she used to know at school and saw in college, asking her about what course she was following. It sounds as if this was not a deliberate carrying out of the homework agreed, but Fran is a very timid, passive girl so we praise her anyway and she looks pleased at this.

Pete says no, nothing special has happened to him, it's all been the same as usual, he hasn't won the pools (loud guffaw at this point). He did engage someone in conversation, though, stopping to talk to the shopkeeper from whom he bought his cigarettes; no problem *here*, it seems.

Jim took the initiative in starting what proved to be quite a long and interesting conversation with a fellow traveller on the train to Bristol two days previously for a job interview. The interview itself proved disappointing, however—he didn't get the job and when we ask him how the interview itself went, and how satisfied he is with his own performance, he says at once that he feels he didn't quite do himself justice in one or two ways and welcomes the suggestion that we might do some work on this, next week perhaps—though he doesn't think he'll feel as nervous as in a "real-life" interview. Mary says she's had a lot of experience of making people uncomfortable in interviews and thinks she can promise to give him a hard time, and everyone laughs. Laughter is an important element in groups like this.

So the leaders bring the group back to the problem with Ronnie's radio, and suggest he role-plays the scene "just as it happened" with John as the shopkeeper. John asks for details about the man: what was he like? where was he—behind a counter? sitting or standing? exactly what did he say? what sort of voice and speech—gruff, abrupt, polite? The scene is played, a very brief one with Ronnie simply asking for his radio and saying "Oh, all right, then" when told it isn't ready yet as the missing part hasn't arrived. After an immediate "Thanks Ronnie, that's a good scene to work on; you've given us a clear picture of what happened", the leaders explore with him what response he would like to make. He insists he does want his set back and (in response to further questioning) that, if the man can't put it right, he wants it back anyway. We discuss and establish the exact words he will say when he goes to the shop again in two days' time, if the radio still isn't ready: "Well, I want it back definitely next week, and if it isn't ready when I come in, I'll take it back anyway". The scene is then rerun twice. On the first occasion Ronnie makes the intended statement but speaking rather quietly, so he is encouraged to repeat it speaking rather louder and with more emphasis. He turns in a good performance and we tell him so.

The group turns next to the situation between Neil and his supervisor, the leaders stressing how easy it is to get into a negative pattern of interaction, with people "sniping" at each other all the time, and they try to explore some more positive, approving kinds of remark which Neil might make to try to introduce a new element. It is a small workplace, with the supervisor also producing work, not simply supervising, so we settle on making an approving comment on a piece of work Bill, the supervisor, has done himself. At first Neil is sceptical and wonders whether Bill will take it amiss or think he is being sarcastic, but after he has role-played it he starts to feel more hopeful and thinks he will try it.

There is time for work on one more situation. The leaders comment that most members want to meet more people and there is some discussion about this. One or two members are anxious that if they talk to people they don't know they might start to give away things about themselves they don't want others to know; Mary tries to reassure Toni in particular about this, and Toni, encouraged, is starting to say something about having been in the local psychiatric hospital, so Mary tells her very clearly (but also very gently) that she will certainly find if she does some work on it that she doesn't have to talk to people about anything she doesn't want to—but that her time in the hospital isn't anything very terrible in any case.

At this point Ronnie starts to say that "If people knew the places I'd been and the things that had happened in my life . . .", to which the leaders respond quickly, "It's quite all right—we don't need to know anything about people's past, we're just content to know you as you are, and we like you because you're a friendly, helpful bloke" —which he certainly was, in the group.

We then return to Toni and set up a simple role-play with her and Fran meeting as strangers at a table in a self-service cafe where, it is assumed, Toni has stopped for a cup of tea while out on a shopping expedition. They start a conversation without difficulty and without any hint of approaching sensitive or embarrassing topics, exchanging details about the part of the city in which they live and chatting about prices in the shops. It is simple enough, but they are two very timid young women and deserve—and receive —approval from the group.

The session ends with agreement on homework assignments. Neil and Ronnie have tasks arising directly out of their role-play; the rest of the group agree to pay a compliment or give a special word of thanks or appreciation to someone, the leaders undertaking to do the same.

The next week's session begins as before with an account from each member of his or her experience during the past week and of how the homework went. Ronnie has managed to state firmly his demand for the return of his radio, repaired or not, the following week and the shopkeeper has assured him that he will have it then (and indeed he did, duly repaired, to Ronnie's great surprise and gratification).

Neil has indeed complimented his supervisor on a piece of work well executed. We ask how Bill received his remark and Neil says he looked a bit taken aback, but then adds that at least things were pleasanter during the week and Bill hasn't picked on him recently, so on the whole he is quite pleased with the experiment and thinks he might try it again.

In the course of these accounts of the past week Fran tells us about an incident with her mother. She had got ready to go out but her mother stopped her and told her to go back and change—Fran likes to dress in modern teenage styles while her mother prefers more conventional clothes. Fran had done so. We enact this scene with Mary playing mother, after Fran has briefed her on how to do it, and Fran acting just as she did at home. Fran's response is an immediate passive compliance, with no protest whatever. The leaders comment that they can see Fran is very fond of her mother, and so wishes to please her, but presumably is dissatisfied with her own (excessive) compliance since she has raised this as a problem. They doubt whether at the present stage Fran could meet such a head-on onslaught from her mother, and say so, but help her to devise an alternative scenario in which she speaks to her mother *before* changing to go out and explains why she wants to wear a particular outfit though she knows her mother prefers others which she does in fact wear on some occasions. This she practises several times, at first with one or two prompts from another of the leaders.

Next, Mary offers to do some work with Jim on his interview. This seems likely to be of limited interest to the rest of the group but we are fortunate in being able to use an adjoining room for it. The last job interview is role-played and Mary, by some very tough questioning, is soon finding that Jim is shifting about on his chair and looking distinctly uneasy. After the first run-through Mary identifies as a major difficulty the way Jim responds when he has to confess that he lacks the experience or qualifications seen as desirable for the post. He tends to become defensive and evasive, but when this is discussed with him is soon able to develop and practise a response which simply admits that particular lack and enables him to move back more confidently as soon as appropriate to areas in which he is more competent. They also work on ways in which he might respond if he is questioned about his extended period of sickness the previous year, since he has already expressed anxiety about having to admit to psychiatric treatment.

In the other part of the group, Pete and Ronnie are practising "getting to know you" talk with Toni and Fran in an imaginary cafeteria. They both have a pleasant manner and do well until Pete asks one of the girls "Like to meet me for a drink tonight?" and follows this with an immediate burst of laughter, which makes it sound as if he is making fun of her. The leaders comment (supported by the girls) that Pete and Ronnie had done fine up to that point, but that some more remains to be done with Pete to help him with his inappropriate laughter. Paul offers to bring a tape-recorder next week which can be used to record role-plays and demonstrate progress and this is accepted without any apparent reluctance since he makes it clear it will only be used as and when people want.

The two parts of the group then come together for the final 10 or 15 minutes of the session during which members agree on home-work for the coming week.

General Comments

This fairly detailed description of the two meetings is intended to illustrate the flexibility of the method and some of the wide range of situations to which it can be applied (there are many others—child management for instance). The leadership style is in some ways very directive, so that it is important (for instance) to invite par-ticipation by saying "Come on, let's . . ." or "Why don't we try . . . ?" rather than "Would you like to . . . ?", but nevertheless each piece of work contains some element of asking "Do you want to do things differently? Would this be an appropriate way for you to tackle it?".

Learning to conduct groups of this kind has three elements. First, it draws heavily on the classic casework/counselling skills described in Chapters 5 to 7, such as empathy, challenge, reassurance, planning and general group skills. Second, students learn to adapt and combine these skills in a simulated group in which they play client roles and take turns in assuming leadership. In such training sessions it is essential to stop frequently to discuss what is happening and what to do next, since students find at first there is simply too much to take into account and keep track of. Above all, they have to be reminded always to reinforce clients immediately after each role-play, as the temptation to offer a critical first comment or accusatory question ("Why didn't you—?") is almost overpowering at times. At the third and final stage, skill and confidence can best be developed by running a group jointly with a more experienced practitioner. Such a progression enables workers to develop what often appears to them at first to be a style of helping at variance with their normal one, and yet it is possible (and helpful) to show that in fact it draws on all their repertoire of existing skills.

CHAPTER 9   Social skills and the group care setting

The previous chapter was concerned with social skills training as practised with groups of people living in the community, hence the people involved were a mixture of different client groups with varying characteristics and life experiences, both past and current; they came from varying backgrounds and might have little in common with each other. In such a setting, group leaders may not have much prior knowledge of members, nor any control over the factors in their environment which may encourage or discourage new learning. None of these facts is likely to apply to social skills training in settings such as residential homes or day centres, and indeed it is work done in such group care settings which is the principal focus of the remaining chapters of this book. Before going on to describe this work, therefore, some attention needs to be given to the effects of the setting itself and to how workers may usefully take account of these and respond to them.

Despite the great variety of client groups and types of institution involved, which can make it seem difficult, perhaps overambitious, to write about group care in general terms, there are a number of problems which workers in residential institutions share—and indeed share not only with each other but also with workers in day care centres of various kinds. We shall, however, presently see that they also share some advantages which are denied to fieldworkers. Current thinking about provision, moreover, seems likely to encourage services to develop in ways which may be much more favourable to social interaction and skills than the traditional kinds of institution.

Aims of Group Care: Are they Likely to Promote or to Undermine Social Skills?

The aim of residential or day care might at one time have been defined broadly in terms of providing people with necessary care which they were unable to receive elsewhere; today we might want to extend this definition so as to cover the offer of experiences designed to enrich their present and possibly their future lives, and perhaps to envisage different forms of group care between which individuals might move as their needs changed. Douglas and Payne (1987), for instance, put forward a concept of group care as characterized by a range and variety of services in which no one form is superior to another: "as an idea it changes the values given to the various forms of service provision". They identify four salient features of any group care setting as:

- Physical environment
- Organization providing the care
- Various activities of daily living
- Social experiences bringing people together

All of these features can exercise an influence on the way clients interact with each other, especially factors like the layout of buildings, arrangements for meals and the organization's practices for consulting clients about decisions which concern them. In similar vein, the Wagner Report (1988) argues, with specific reference to residential provision, that: "Where accommodation and services are combined, they should have a clearly defined purpose and should be fully integrated, philosophically and organisationally, into the wider spectrum of service provision to which they relate. We use the term group living to denote those arrangements whereby accommodation and services are integrated to enable groups of people with some identified assumed or real common needs *to live interdependently*" (our emphasis).

Davis (1982) places the fostering of appropriate dependence, independence and interdependence at the head of his list of the social work tasks involved in residential care and acknowledges that: "By its very nature residential living militates against the encouragement of independent thought and action . . . . It takes only a little while for a resident to lose the will to think and act independently, and for staff to regard as disruptive a person who will not allow this to happen". He later adds that; "Social skills not acquired as part of the earlier developmental process are less likely to come naturally following admission to a residential home. Opportunities may be lessened, and failure in some activities may result in ridicule". It might be added that where social skills, even though practised at a former life stage, have been allowed to atrophy, as they might in the case of an elderly person living alone, they may well not be re-established without help after admission to group care.

The notion of enriching people's lives may imply not only the willingness to do things for them but also a belief in their own capacity for change. People can change, adapt and develop even in an almost static environment and this ability is of central importance for conserving a sense of personal identity, integrity and autonomy, in other words for maintaining a sense of self-worth. There is an intimate relationship between this capacity for change and the sense of self-worth; each is essential to the other. Of course, a bad institution can cause people to change for the worse, to lose capacities which they had on admission so that their lives are thereby impoverished, but it is all too easy to assume that any change will necessarily mean deterioration. Such a pessimistic view is challenged by the growing practice of admitting elderly people to residential care for strictly limited periods in order to build up their autonomy and their capabilities and then discharge them to independent living. The process of institutionalization, insidious and pervasive though it may be, is certainly not inevitable, and its progress can be countered—and indeed even reversed—by staff who encourage residents to develop and practise their social skills within a general programme designed to combat apathy and dependency.

The Care Setting: Help or Hindrance to Social Skills Training?

Group care settings offer advantages for social skills development in some respects, but in others they present drawbacks. An immediate advantage lies in the fact that workers in such a setting are likely to have a special knowledge both of their particular client group and (probably) of individual clients within it far exceeding that of most fieldworkers. This is particularly true where severe physical or intellectual impairment is concerned, as we were reminded recently while helping a staff member at a day care centre for severely handicapped young adults to set up a social skills project with a group of clients at the centre. The clients in question were wheelchair-bound, had little control of their limbs and severe learning difficulties and some lacked speech almost entirely. The worker's patient and sensitive attention, together with his familiarity with the individual clients and their confidence in him, enabled him to communicate with them and to achieve remarkable progress in a situation in which we were both helpless; indeed, it would not have occurred to us that it would be possible to undertake such a piece of work. We were able to provide the methodology, but all the vital skills belonged to the worker. While this special expertise is a valuable asset, it does of course have its dangers: if you yourself can understand a client with a speech defect without difficulty, you may forget that others meeting him for the first time may find some sentences unintelligible.

Workers in such specialized settings are clearly well equipped to carry out assessments and evaluate progress, indeed the settings themselves often have useful assessment material available even before a particular project is commenced. They will know what situations are likely to crop up in which newly acquired skills can be practised without having to elicit these from clients (who indeed may not know of them) and will be able to identify or suggest appropriate kinds of reinforcers. These resources of knowledge and experience provide a valuable perspective on the clients to be utilized within the wider context of group living, which can, from the social skills standpoint, be conceived as an archway into wider, richer spheres of activity.

A further strength of group care situations is their potential for offering or developing natural peer groups. A worker may already know several clients who would form a natural working group. The importance of peer group support and approval has already been stressed (and illustrated in the last chapter), and group care situations offer many opportunities for providing and fostering such support. Many of the problems that beset individuals may be most effectively tackled in the context of this kind of peer group. Existing relationships in the setting are necessarily an important factor in making the decision whether to work on an individual or a group basis. Strong, positive relationships give the worker a head start but on the other hand there may be personal antagonisms, or divisions based on group loyalties. This would be particularly likely to obtain in an institution such as a children's home, where the authority component of the staff role is particularly explicit. Here, the worker's overall role in relation to the clients might interfere with any attempt to work with them on a social skills programme. Moreover, little can be achieved without the help and collaboration of other staff members. Securing this cooperation is an absolute prerequisite for setting up the work with the client, and while this may sound a straightforward matter, it can actually prove more difficult to secure the collaboration of colleagues than that of clients.

Such negative factors may be encountered singly or in combination and their effect may be compounded by a prevailing atmosphere in which dependency is fostered and initiative undermined—a climate which staff and clients collude in producing. Even so, a worker who is really committed to helping clients to interact in a way which better satisfies their needs can often overcome the difficulties involved, and here an outside consultant who is a specialist in the method can give a great deal of valuable support and advice. It is surprising what can be accomplished, given this commitment and outside help, even in settings which initially appeared unpromising.

To return to the positive features, the group care setting itself may offer learning opportunities and the chance to practise newly acquired skills without all the doubtful and risky factors which may be involved outside an environment which is familiar to clients and reasonably predictable. The worker will know who are the other members of staff whom the client may be approaching with a request and may, if necessary, prepare these colleagues to respond in particular ways. It is reasonable to hope that consistency and continuity of work are more likely to be ensured in such a setting, where clients and other staff are often accessible at more frequent intervals. Such considerations are particularly important in a method of work which proceeds by small incremental shifts and gains. Similar advantages may apply in the evaluation of the programme, though if the clients in question have moved on elsewhere a special effort often needs to be made to see whether gains have been maintained—and this is not always possible. But the group setting itself clearly offers possibilities for a variety of people (staff and peers as well as family and friends) to take part in monitoring and assessing progress on a continuing basis.

Social Skills and Institutionalization

Decreasing autonomy and self-reliance and increasing helpless-ness are frequently the reason for which care is offered to clients but, by a well-documented paradox, they may actually be exacer-bated by the care that is given. Some of the effects of segregat-ing handicapped children in a protected environment are dis-cussed in Chapter 11; with elderly people the effect can be even more dramatic. It is often quicker and easier to do things for people than to encourage and support them in fending for themselves, and thus the process of regression and the consequent lack of inde-pendence may be fostered by care staff who unthinkingly collude with clients in shedding their everyday responsibilities. In some residential situations a period of regression may be a necessary prerequisite for later progress, but this should not preclude helping people to overcome any communication problems they may be experiencing.

As an illustration, staff in elderly persons' homes often become aware of problems of relationships and interaction between two or more residents, or between residents and their families, which they may then take action to resolve without considering the alternative possibility of enabling the resident to take the necessary initiative. The three following examples, all provided by residential staff working with elderly clients, illustrate this choice, underlining the fact that staff do not have to take responsibility for ironing out all residents' problems.

> Bill, an 80-year-old widower, resented the fact that his daughter took charge of his pension, leaving him no spending money and simply bringing in a few things for him occasionally when she judged he needed them. The manager originally intended to approach the daughter on the subject herself, but eventually she—and Bill—decided that it would be better for him, after a few rehearsals, to open the subject himself. In the event, this approach probably worked better than that originally envisaged, since it seemed likely that the daughter would have regarded it as "interference".

Mrs Carson was a confused lady in her late seventies who had difficulty remembering where her own room was and so often went into a neighbouring room by mistake. If this happened at night it could be quite frightening to be suddenly woken up by Mrs Carson's entry and the other resident would usually call the duty staff member in some distress. After discussion the manager started to consider the alternative approach of teaching the neighbour a strategy for dealing with the intrusion herself. This approach had the enormous advantage of enabling the neighbour to feel much more in control of the situation.

Tom, in his early eighties, seemed unusually morose, and when a care assistant asked him what was bothering him replied that the "rather superior" new resident had taken his favourite chair. He doesn't want to cause any trouble, he says, but would she—or "matron"—please tell her about it? The care assistant and manager together set up a simple role-play with Tom, and at the end of two or three repetitions he decided that he could handle the situation himself, and would in fact prefer to do so.

There are, then, many situations in which a simple shaping technique such as that used in the above examples may be employed to restore a resident's autonomy. It is of great value that clients should be enabled to make reasonable requests, refuse unreasonable demands and generally exercise as much choice and discrimination as possible. An encouraging development in both residential and day care is the setting up of client groups to carry out a particular task—making some decision of common interest for instance—or to work in a particular way, but many staff express doubts about their clients' ability to take any real part in these activities. Many clients have indeed been conditioned into passive and inarticulate behaviour, sometimes over a period of years, and will need help in recovering their former skills as well as acquiring new ones. This is particularly relevant in work with elderly and with mentally handicapped clients, among whom the level of interaction in group care settings is often strikingly low. While the more usual targets chosen for social skills training programmes may be interaction with people outside the immediate group, another type of programme may be designed with the aim of building up the rate and quality of interaction within the group itself.

Sally, a care assistant in an elderly persons' home, set up a small discussion-type group comprising four elderly men. Working with very simple prompting and modelling techniques, she shaped a considerable increase in interaction both in the "rate of chat" and in the quality of the conversation. Encouraged by this, she asked her clients if she could bring in a video camera and record some sessions. They thought this a good idea and found it enjoyable and amusing, joking together about being "film stars". The overall effect on these elderly men, who had previously been quite reticent and withdrawn, was very positive and actually brought about a significant improvement in the quality of life they were able to enjoy. It is important to remember that for the newly learned behaviour to be maintained it must be accompanied by new, more positive ways of thinking about oneself; not, that is, as an unwanted, useless old man, but as a social being capable of making and enjoying friendships (Meichenbaum 1977; Trower 1984).

Situations of this kind are frequent and simple programmes of the kind just described are not difficult to set up, yet social skills training is a method of work very little used with elderly clients though it clearly has a great deal to offer them. There are, however, two increasingly popular methods of working with groups of elderly clients which have certain affinities with social skills training and could well be used in conjunction with it: these are reality orientation and reminiscence therapy. Reality orientation uses a variety of means to call people's attention to the present situation and their immediate surroundings, the date and time, the weather and season of the year, and so on. The aim is to counter the numbing effect of the institution, which tends to insulate its residents from the outside world to the point where they cease to be aware of it. Staff not only draw residents' attention to the date and the weather but encourage them to respond, thereby at the same time keeping them in touch with reality and promoting conversation and interaction. Reminiscence therapy makes use of the familiar fact that old people, even when their short-term memory is very poor, often remember their early life with quite astonishing vividness. Group sessions are arranged in the course of which the participants can share reminiscences of events in the distant past at either national or local level or exchange memories about episodes in their personal lives. Projects may also be set up to assemble collections of old photographs, domestic utensils or other souvenirs which illustrate what life was like for these clients 50, 60 or 70 years ago. Such programmes can help withdrawn or confused elderly people to express themselves and to feel that they and their memories are valued; indeed, the clients themselves will be the experts on the subjects in question, about which the worker will have no first-hand experience. Reminiscence therapy, then, can be particularly valuable through its potential for improving clients' self-image and, even more than reality orientation, it fosters communication and interaction.

The way in which such approaches may be linked to social skills training and the appropriate point at which to make such a transition are immensely variable and call for the same kind of sensitive appraisal which we have put forward as an essential feature of social skills work: is this what the clients want? is it the right time? are the circumstances favourable? what consequences can be expected? Many clients have a need for dependency and passivity at particular stages of their lives; this is quite normal and positive. Crisis theorists have noted that after the impact of a major life crisis most people need to regress and become dependent for a period. This may well be the case with a client after the trauma surrounding admission to residential care if the admission involves a whole succession of losses, with the need for care arising from the progressive loss of physical and psychological capacities and perhaps bereavement as well.

Dependency and Reciprocity

Staff working in group care settings have to recognize dependency and to tolerate and contain it at an acceptable level. Moving forward from this dependency is a highly individual matter, and some clients who have been damaged by neglect, isolation or destructive behaviour may need to be allowed, even encouraged, to regress before they can move on, while others arrive conditioned to dependency by people who need them to be like this. With the elderly—the largest client group in residential care—there is usually an assumption that dependency will inevitably increase, an assumption which may in fact be unwarranted. Davis (1982) maintains that people going into residential care have to make the transition from initial dependency to increasing autonomy through a stage of interdependence. He emphasizes the essentially reciprocal nature of significant relationships, commenting that, in many residential settings, organizational structures and role requirements militate against this reciprocity. He observes, however, that opportunities do exist for reciprocity in relationships between staff and residents: "It is a unique experience to move with a resident from a position as a subordinate object— and, if we are honest, we know that many residents always remain in this state, however we attempt to disguise the fact—to that of a completely accepted person where role differences no longer exist".

The concept of interdependence is a part of the value system underlying good practice in social skills training, which in essence is a means of enabling individuals to meet their own needs more effectively by enhancing their perceptions and their skills of communication. Social skills training can be effective only if client and worker cooperate in the process. This holds true even with severely handicapped or disadvantaged clients, with whom it is still possible to see a genuine consent as a minimum requirement. Where clients have learning difficulties so severe that it is difficult for them to envisage what a programme would involve merely on the basis of an advance explanation, it is simple to mount a trial session and then test their response at the end to see if they want to continue. Their manifest enthusiasm is usually evidence enough.

There is, of course, a particular danger, arising out of the degree of control which staff in a residential setting are able to exert over the environment, that they may be tempted to set up programmes of social skills training as a method of conditioning conformity and compliance. Clearly any such development must be deplored. Fortunately, however, there is little evidence of this happening in practice, since, as has been emphasized, clients do not make progress through the use of these methods unless they are themselves motivated to do so and gain some advantage thereby.

It may be useful here to consider the case of two adolescents in residential care. John is a 16-year-old who responds to fairly mild criticism or censure (or anything which he interprets as such) by rapidly losing his temper and shouting abuse and threats at the staff member concerned. His 17-year-old friend Roy in a similar situation makes no attempt to explain his position and manifests a sullen, silent intransigence throughout. Both boys are making learned responses which are unhelpful both to themselves and to others.

Either response may be functional to some extent in that it maintains a distance, albeit in antagonistic terms, between resident and staff. The approach to the difficulties experienced by these two boys may be different according to the relationships they already have, how often the incidents occur and how long they last, and according to the elements already discussed of dependency level and pace at which they are capable of moving forward. What is certain, however, is that each needs to learn a better appreciation of how he responds and some new, more constructive ways of behaving. He will then have the choice whether or not to use the newly learned behaviour.

In neither of these situations is the goal one of developing passivity or compliance; indeed, in Roy's case, the objective is to enable him to argue his case quite forcibly, albeit with moderation. Teaching an acceptable, appropriate level of assertiveness is an important way of enabling both residents to stand up for themselves in future life, and the utility of this is highlighted by the example cited in Chapter 10 of work with boys in a short-stay children's home.

One method used in social skills training which very much stresses the element of reciprocity is the use of reverse role-play. Where a client's behaviour causes offence to other people, a useful way of helping him to become aware of the effect it arouses is to reverse the roles in a simulated example so that he is himself placed in the position of having to cope with the behaviour which he exhibits. It is important in such simulations to aim for as fair a facsimile as possible in reproducing the behaviour and not to go over the top, and video is a useful aid.

Social Skills and Life Skills

A recurring question which particularly characterizes social skills work in the group care setting is thus: for whose benefit is the programme being undertaken? This question arises, moreover, not only in relation to behaviour which may be deemed to be antisocial but also in the area of the sometimes diffuse and imprecise boundary between social skills and life skills.

We defined social skills at the outset of this book as essentially involving interaction between individuals. A social skill is thus necessarily interpersonal, not simply any skill which is deemed to be socially desirable. The rationale for teaching skills which are truly social in nature is that this will lead to greater satisfaction in personal relationships for the individual as well as for others with whom this individual interacts. This rationale, however, will not necessarily apply to what is taught in many programmes of "social training" for mentally handicapped clients, such as bed-making and money-counting. Similar activities practised in a group care setting could, however, provide the material for learning social skills. Thus, while bed-making in itself is not a social skill, learning to collaborate with someone else to carry out the operation jointly could well be. Similarly, counting money is itself a solitary occupation but could lead on to asking someone else to clarify a monetary transaction or even to challenging someone on whether the correct change has been given. Such purely mechanistic training illustrates the worst potential of old-style behaviour modification and to keep training on this level is selling the clients short. To adopt an approach of this kind is to treat people as less than human and to ignore the vital aspect of thought processes, of individuals' perceptions of them-selves—their self-image—and sense of self-respect, aspects which are heavily dependent on the way other people treat them and respond to them.

Group Care and Self-Image

Apart from its potential for increasing dependency, the group care situation can also affect people's social performance by its effect on their self-image, by virtue of the fact that it places them very explicitly in a given category. Clients can be tacitly invited to see themselves as essentially clients needing care from staff members rather than as individuals experiencing interaction and making and enjoying relationships with each other. We gave an example earlier of work undertaken to improve the level and quality of interaction between residents in an elderly persons' home. In similar vein, Anita, a worker in a day centre, noticed how little casual conversa-tion was occurring between trainees and was successful in motivat-ing and equipping them by a programme of skills training to in-crease their interaction and to improve its quality, and hence also to increase the satisfaction and enjoyment they gained from attending the centre. It seems, moreover, particularly important (Sinclair 1971) that residents in settings like that of a probation hostel should feel able to talk about their feelings—something which requires not only a caring, warm relationship but also the means of expressing the feelings in question. A resident who is so inarticulate that he lacks the appropriate means to express emotions like anger or resentment is likely to act them out in aggressive or destructive behaviour.

A potent impediment to undertaking any new enterprise is the fear of failure and anxiety about its consequences. This fear is often accompanied by negative thoughts of an unrealistic and destructive kind such as "I could never do that", "I was awful" or "I'm a failure". Care staff who are embarking on social skills work need to realize that some such thoughts are likely to be passing through their clients' minds and perhaps check with them just what they are telling themselves, possibly suggesting other, more hopeful messages. Suggestions of this kind can prove surprisingly potent.

An amusing example of this occurred in a mixed social skills group in which Tim, a tall, gangling young man of 22, complained that nobody took any notice of him—and indeed his manner was very unassertive. In role-plays he generally performed in a rather timid and hesitant manner, though his voice and his non-verbal communication improved a little with practice. At one point the group leaders proposed working on an imaginary situation in which the task was to ask a man standing at a railway station to move his small child back away from the edge of the platform, and Tim began in his usual timid fashion, though improving somewhat when he was reminded of the danger to the child. The real breakthrough occurred, however, when he was told to imagine that he was a railway porter, and this time he assumed a commanding voice and manner and ordered the passenger to hold the child out of harm's way. This performance was a revelation to all concerned, not least to Tim himself, so that it was possible to make use of this piece of learning in other subsequent episodes.

A Climate to Foster Social Skills and Interaction

In work with clients who suffer such high levels of anxiety and social inhibition we have to start from small beginnings. A lot of work may be needed at individual level before the client is exposed to group activity. The group care setting may itself offer opportunities for such individual work in small but frequent encounters designed to encourage and build confidence—opportunities such as do not occur in fieldwork. Some clients may decide they do not want to join a group so that work, often very slow and repetitious, has to be continued on an individual basis.

While it may be hoped that such a client will be able ultimately to practise new or enhanced skills in an open environment, we should still want to argue that work of this kind is worth doing for its own sake. If the client feels more competent and confident because of a small growth in capacity in a fairly restricted situation the work still has its value, although it might be difficult to evaluate objectively. Skills, moreover, tend to cluster and coalesce, and improvements in one area often bring considerable benefits in others—the so-called "avalanche effect". One may also reasonably hope for a kind of "secondary avalanche"—the fact that one or two clients in a group setting become more vocal and communicative can stimulate the responses and interaction of others.

This brings us back to a topic touched on at the beginning of the chapter: the design and furnishing of residential institutions (and day centres) as a significant factor in the experience of their clients. The way furniture is arranged in particular can either damp down or foster interaction between residents and it is important that layout should be such that conversations can be entered into easily and naturally rather than having to be set up artificially.

A residential home—or day centre—whose operation is designed to encourage social skills and interaction will be one where care is given on the Miller and Gwynne (1972) "horticultural" model, that is, encouraging the development of latent and neglected capacities and minimizing the recognition of handicap or abnormality. In the case of an old people's home, it will, among Clough's six types of home, resemble the therapeutic unit, in which staff encourage resident participation in terms such as: "You don't have to but I'd like you to join in"; "It's good for you"; and "If you just sit, you'll lose the ability to walk". Here, staff will not wear uniforms, jobs will overlap and units tend to be small, and the head of home is likely to have social work training—or, we would add, other professional training which stresses the development of interpersonal skills.

"Residents are encouraged to be independent and to try to perform tasks, and the attempt is seen as valuable in itself" (Clough 1981). Indeed, whatever the care setting or the client group for which it caters, the style and atmosphere which will most favour social interaction and skills development will be precisely those which in general terms can be seen as fostering the individuality and autonomy of clients.

CHAPTER 10   Social skills training with children and adolescents

A setting in which it can readily be seen that social skills training has a great deal to offer is the residential care of children and adolescents, since these are clients who are generally perceived as learning new attitudes and behaviour all the time—that is, even when the experience of learning is not deliberately structured. For this very reason, the ethical issues around the question of who is to benefit from any programme of training are likely to be particularly sensitive and easy to overlook. Some practitioners feel that in some statutory institutions—closed units in particular—it is not possible for participation to be genuinely voluntary, and hence they would not set up social skills training programmes in such a setting. This is, of course, a special case of the more general question of whether it is proper to use behavioural methods generally in a situation which the client has not entered of his own free will. Those who would oppose their use unequivocally seem to be arguing that any behavioural methods are equivalent to the use of supposedly irresistible behaviour modification and that this amounts to unjustifiable manipulation and arbitrary social control. This argument has been advanced in the social work context by Epstein (1975), who refers to behaviour modification as "the new cool-out therapy", that is, simply a more effective method of social control. However, the experience of running social skills groups, albeit in a context of containment, will show that clients are able even there to identify new behaviour which they want to learn for their own sake and, in any case, they will not in fact continue to practise any new behaviour they have learned unless they gain some advantage from doing so. The work of Priestley et al (1978, 1984) has demonstrated that it is possible to offer clients something which they can use even in the unpromising setting of prison. They comment that "in prisons it is perfectly possible to create self-contained islands of choice and co-operation where the ordinary rules and disciplines of the institution are inoperative" (Priestley et al 1978).

In any residential child care setting it is always a factor, albeit an implicit one, that the staff are in positions of authority in relation to the children, and frequently this authority is actually explicit. Nowhere is this more evident than in closed units for disturbed or delinquent children, where staff often have misgivings about offering any programme of social training, especially one incorporating a system of rewards or "inducements", in a situation which is essentially one of confinement. Even in an open children's home similar doubts may arise, and may be compounded by the assessment and evaluation function in work in short-stay homes where the children's future destiny may be at stake. It is somewhat like the difficulty raised earlier in connection with professional skills: we are asking people to admit to and explore difficulties in social performance with people who are going to make some kind of judgement on them and their abilities in these areas. There is perhaps here a link with the problem issue highlighted by Carl Rogers (1942) that therapy and authority cannot be coexistent in the same relationship. But social skills training is not therapy; it is basically about learning, and we can all recall experiences of learning from people holding authority over us—our own parents not least. A final question must, however, be settled in the mind before a skills programme is embarked upon. Is it envisaged to foster the smooth running of the establishment or the interests of the clients?

The programme which we are about to describe was in fact carried out in a short-stay children's home situated near a small country town. The worker concerned was Stan, a young houseparent nearing the end of his in-service professional training, who had an excellent relationship with the boys in his care and showed himself to be particularly sensitive to the pressures and constraints on their autonomy. The success of the work is due less to a detailed knowledge of theory than to his ability to apply the theoretical approach in a sensitive and imaginative way.

PROGRAMME WITH A GROUP OF THREE BOYS— PROBLEM IDENTIFICATION AND DEFINITION

Stan began by looking at the records of some of the boys to see what indications these offered of problem areas which they might be motivated to work on. The way a number of the comments were expressed gave rise to some concern in him—indeed, it is a familiar phenomenon in assessment units of various kinds that the procedures for assessment and the methods of recording it tend to skew the thoughts and feelings of professional staff about their clients in particular directions. In Stan's view, the actual instruments encouraged people to express particular feelings which, as he put it, "could become facts, because of the power of the written word". His principal concern, however, was the lack of consultation and involvement of clients in the process. He found the approach of Priestley et al (1978) particularly helpful here:

> . . . this approach is intended to appeal directly to the people with the problems and to put into their hands the tools they need to dig themselves out of the holes they are in. It aims to equip them with the means of surviving more successfully in complex, urban environments: to communicate effectively, for instance, to make good decisions to handle difficult social situations, to set and achieve personal goals—to assume, in other words, a measure of control and self-direction over the course of their own lives.

Stan began his preparation for setting up a programme by spending a few days observing the social behaviour of the boys with special attention, and he was struck by the frequency with which a number of the boys (three in particular) completely lost their tempers, sometimes with staff members but more usually with other boys. He saw that such incidents often led to the boys concerned getting into some form of trouble and becoming very distressed and tearful, subsequently going to great lengths to make some kind of reparation for their outburst, all of which suggested that this behaviour was something they regretted and would be glad to be able to control more effectively. He checked his perceptions with other members of staff and then went on to look more closely at one particular boy, Neil, who seemed to be displaying the most marked problems, constructing a simple chart for him on a daily basis with space to enter an indication of his mood on a five-point scale at suitable intervals. The scale ran:

1. Temper outburst with loss of control
2. Short flare-up/irritability

3. Bad mood
4. Very minor upset, quick recovery
5. Even-tempered

Alongside the rating scale were columns providing for the classic behavioural data:

What happened?
When did it happen (time—what else was happening)?
Who was involved?
Where did it happen?
Why did it happen? (staff perception)

At the end of a week he transferred the data on to a graph and under this he inserted the information derived from the replies to the above questions. The graph served two main purposes: first it provided factual information on the frequency of Neil's outburst, and secondly it pinpointed the people and situations involved. It was, in fact, a useful baseline from which to plan and evaluate future progress.

The home's records on Neil were, on the other hand, far from encouraging in their general tenor. Neil had been admitted for a full assessment at the age of 13, having committed several offences, showing serious problems in his school situation and being beyond his mother's control. He was perceived by staff as being self-confident ("bumptious"), refusing to accept authority, argumentative and abusive. He associated with several other boys who were also perceived as brash and aggressive. In the classroom he was seen as "sullen, aggressive with a quick temper, liable to act without thought of the consequences of his actions". The recommendations were for "long-term training within a residential establishment".

Stan next had an individual talk with Neil, in which he suggested that he should complete a target-type chart designed to highlight aspects of social behaviour. In this test, the subject rates himself on a five-point scale in relation to a number of factors; a dot for each factor is then entered at the appropriate position on the target chart. Neil's chart is reproduced in Figure 10.1.

The advantage of setting the results out in this way is that the presentation is very clear and easily grasped by the subject. Stan discussed this chart with Neil and how he felt about it. Neil said he

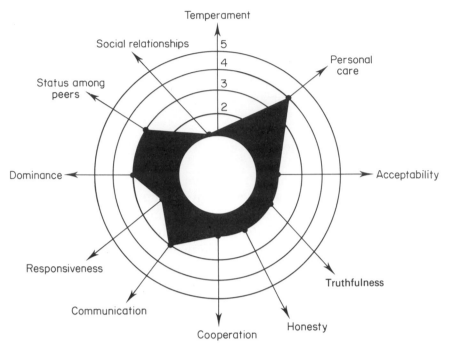

Figure 10.1. Target chart: Neil's profile. The qualities shown were identified jointly as significant by worker and client. Temperament refers to ability to avoid/control temper loss. A high score indicates a good performance level, a low score a problem one

could see clearly that the area of "temperament" caused him problems; his lack of temper control was a major trouble and worry to him and he always felt bad after he had lost control of himself. In the discussion he mentioned other boys as having the same problem, naming them as David (14) and Andrew (13). Stan explained that he thought there were some ways in which he could help Neil with this difficulty of his and went on to suggest that they might like to join Neil and form a small group in which the three boys could work on this together, a suggestion which Neil welcomed. Stan reminded Neil that he was on a course and that this involved him in learning about new ways of doing things himself, so he certainly was not making any pretence of expertise in a method which in fact was new to him. Most people, he said, felt like losing their temper at times, but some of them managed to find ways of controlling it a bit better than others and the group would be trying to find out and learn about the secrets or skills of keeping control of your temper. He finished by thanking Neil for doing the test and he and Neil agreed to meet again to talk about the next stage in a few days' time. Subsequently he went through a similar process of interview and personal assessment with David and Andrew, who also proved keen to do some work on temper control.

Setting up the Group

Stan then held a meeting with the three boys to talk about the way he thought the group might set about learning. He mentioned an idea which he had discussed with his tutor and study supervisor: to choose another boy to join the group whom these boys themselves identified as being good at controlling his temper and avoiding getting involved in rows and who could help to monitor progress and serve as a model. The three boys thought about this and suggested Martin, another 13-year-old; Martin agreed to join the group and completed a chart of his own. It was vital that this boy was the group's own choice, that is, someone they perceived as having the skills appropriate for them.

Stan then asked four of his staff colleagues to complete personal assessments for each of the four boys, using the same method. He found some divergences from the way the boys had assessed themselves but in general temperament and personality ratings showed a surprising degree of agreement. Stan did not have the time to prepare a baseline chart for the other boys as he had done for Neil and regretted this; it meant that evaluating progress could be done more accurately in Neil's case. The programme was drawn up by discussion between Stan and the boys, one of the first things they needed to decide being the choice of devices to monitor progress and of suitable incentives to motivate the group. It was decided that the boys should keep individual star charts, each boy being responsible for his own. The purposes of the charts were:

- To set personal objectives
- To enable individual boys to see their own progress
- To keep a record of progress for the group
- To provide for reinforcement with linked rewards (plus verbal praise and encouragement)

- To highlight the critical periods of the day and pinpoint individual problem situations
- To provide homework, the completion of the charts functioning to remind the boys of the programme and to foster generalization

The group met one morning a week, with meetings lasting most of the morning and continuing over a short period of only five weeks. This was an unusual format, brought about by the constraints of the working practices of the establishment and of the project which Stan had to prepare and submit on his course, and it is not one that would have been recommended, as such long sessions could easily pall, with all the momentum and enthusiasm dissipating. In the present instance, however, Stan's own enthusiasm and his remarkable flair for working with these boys entirely precluded any such effect.

At the first full meeting Stan began by reminding the boys of the purpose of the programme, and also that he was on a course and exploring new ways of trying to help people with their problems. He outlined the basic methods which would be used: discussion and role-plays through which they could practise and watch how other people tackled things. He then gave an outline for this first morning. First came a "brainstorming" session, in which Stan wrote down all the things which the boys brought up as making them lose their tempers; these they agreed to call "triggers". The list was formidable: pushing, bumping, name-calling, people refusing to share, not having enough time or space, being beaten in a contest, and many more. Next, Stan asked the boys to pick actual incidents which had occurred, and several of these were briefly role-played in illustration. He encouraged them to talk about what it feels like to lose your temper, not only the emotions experienced but the physical sensations such as pounding heart, tenseness, dryness in the throat, shaking and quivering. Stan helped them to make some connections with other situations which aroused similar sensations, mainly those which caused them anxiety or made them fear loss of control. The discussion moved on to the consequences of losing your temper and Stan produced newspaper cuttings to illustrate some of the dire results that could follow. All this gave an added emphasis to the boys' wish to develop strategies of self-control.

Stan's next suggestion was that the group might invite Jane, one of the housemothers, to participate for part of the sequence, as she might have a contribution to make. As the group agreed to this, Jane joined them and talked about how hard she found it to keep her own temper at times and about how she contrived to manage it (but only just!). She mentioned particularly keeping cool in arguments and disputes, and at Stan's suggestion the two of them role-played an example of this for the boys—an excellent illustration of the "everyone has problems of this sort" element in the social skills approach which can play such a valuable part in encouraging an optimistic start on the work. The boys went on to role-play some simple situations themselves with some reinforcement in the form of sweets, using some of the incidents Stan had observed in his baseline observations, and he was struck by how naturally and readily the boys took to the role-plays and how much they enjoyed them.

At the end of the first meeting, Stan reverted to the subject of the stars (token reinforcers) and how they would like to use them, the stars being awarded both for performance in group sessions and for periods free of temper outbursts during the rest of the week. Discussion between the boys led to the following scale, derived from the preferences they expressed:

10 stars: half an hour of Stan's time for games
10 stars: use of Stan's radio or tape-player for one evening
15 stars: a walk up to the woods to play
15 stars: bag of sweets, or chocolate bar
15 stars: airgun shooting
20 stars: visit to town for cup of coffee or tea
20 stars: half-hour on the centre's motor-cycle
20 stars: extensive pillion ride on Stan's motor-cycle

The morning finished with Stan praising the group for the effort they had put in and clarifying once again how they were to keep their progress charts.

Progress, Outcome and Comments on the Programme

Subsequent groups followed the same general format as the first one, with a recurrent mix, that is, of explanations, demonstration, modelling, role-play and discussion, reinforcement being contingent on maintaining and improving performance. The star charts proved to be an intrinsic form of reinforcement in themselves through the satisfaction the boys gained from simply contemplating this concrete evidence of their progress. Stan commented: "It has become apparent to me that the star charts, sweets and chat at the end of the day would have been quite sufficient in rewarding and reinforcing the control of temper, ever though they said they would like to do things like ride the motor-bike as rewards; only a little time has been spent in the last three or four weeks on activities such as this, and then sometimes at my instigation. The boys have always been eager to show me how well they have done at the end of the day, and in retrospect this may have been reward enough". It was always crucial to the success of this programme that the boys had a warm relationship with Stan, realized how genuine was his concern for them and their happiness, and had a growing belief that it was possible to change behaviour by the methods being used.

The evaluation of this short programme comprised reratings of the charts made at the outset by boys and staff and of Neil's performance and progress (as illustrated in Figure 10.1). The progress made by the three was generally very encouraging, though Stan thought that Neil and Andrew showed a better response overall than did David. Interestingly, when he made some follow-up enquiries after the boys were transferred, he found that the gains achieved had in fact been well maintained. Neil in particular had done remarkably well, and indeed staff at the home to which he had moved expressed scepticism about the temper problems noted on his record—they did not perceive that he had any such problem. Equally encouraging was the boys' immediate response to the programme, which was to ask whether they could tackle some more problems in the group in a similar way.

To mount such a successful programme within the constraints which were operating the worker needed an excellent sense of timing and pace. While it would usually be considered preferable to set up a series of perhaps 10 sessions lasting not more than an hour and a half, in this instance we are looking at a sequence lasting over a period only half this and with about double the normal duration. It was only because Stan was such an effective worker and so capable of engaging the boys' interest and enthusiasm that he was able to make a success of it; with some client groups it would probably not be feasible to keep the momentum going for such a long stretch.

It is often not possible for workers in the caring services to evaluate the outcome of their work as Stan did, and certainly this can seldom be done as rigorously as would be expected in the practice of clinical psychology. The other case illustrations to be described will demonstrate some of the obstacles to a stringent evaluation. Sometimes the client will be moving on to circumstance in which a follow-up inquiry could be intrusive; this may be the case where a child in care goes home to a rather hostile family situation. Again, it is not always possible to rely on the objectivity of the principal observers (the worker and colleagues), in that they may be too ready to infer favourable changes or too sceptical about them, or they may be biased by what they have read in the client's record. Nevertheless, a conscientious worker will make every effort to keep track of the effectiveness of any programme. This is part of the feedback which we all need to help us augment and refine our own professional skills.

While social skills training is often a very attractive option in work with children precisely because of the emphasis on doing rather than talking, often a great deal of work needs to be done by other methods: counselling, for instance, may form a very important part of the work with disturbed children. Once the social skills programme itself has begun, however, the accent needs to be on movement and progress; in any case, a lot of cognitive restructuring can go on during the role-plays and the intervals between them. Our next case example is an illustration of how work based on role-play and rehearsal can be integrated with a more insight-oriented approach, although for this to be a real possibility a one-to-one situation is usually needed. If it is attempted in a group setting, this will have the effect of slowing progress and hence losing the momentum for change and perhaps inducing apathy in the group members not immediately involved.

WORK WITH A 15-YEAR-OLD GIRL: DEFINING THE PROBLEM

The setting is again a short-stay children's home, this time in a provincial city. The worker is Valerie, a young housemother, and the client is 15-year-old Miranda, who, after considerable problems at home, was waiting to attend court in the near future for offences committed while she was in care. Since being in the home she had encountered a number of difficulties with staff, other youngsters and people outside. Valerie herself had established an easy, non-directive relationship with Miranda, who responded well to friendly interest and advice. Valerie realized that Miranda was rather preoccupied with aspects of her appearance and behaviour, and that allied to this preoccupation were feelings of inferiority and a tendency to stereotype other people according to their role, age and gender. One particularly worrying manifestation was her aggressive behaviour towards people she thought were talking about her and laughing at her. Valerie considered that Miranda needed help with this as a matter of some urgency, as there had been recent incidents in which she had assaulted people in the street. Valerie did not think, however, that Miranda was intrinsically violent or that the behaviour was a consequence of any form of mental illness, and on reflection she concluded that the girl had a depressed self-image which had developed from her negative self-perceptions and led to feelings of inadequacy about her ability to relate to others and to exercise control over situations. Miranda's low level of self-assertion brought about depressed feelings of resentment and these in turn led to incidents of very excessive behaviour, as in the recent violent outbursts. The sequence is illustrated in Figure 10.2.

Valerie talked to Miranda, discussing this pattern of behaviour and offering to spend some time with her on a regular basis to see if she could help her. Miranda agreed readily; again it is important to recognize that the client was accepting help from a member of staff with whom she already had an established relationship of mutual trust and regard.

Assessment took three main forms. Initially, Valerie used her short sessions with Miranda not only to encourage and motivate her but also to identify those situations and people which she found most threatening; secondly, Miranda completed a simple questionnaire for her; thirdly, she drew on observations by other staff. The results were clear-cut: Miranda's problems mainly involved authority situations with people whom she regarded as of high status. There were also difficulties in areas where some degree of assertiveness

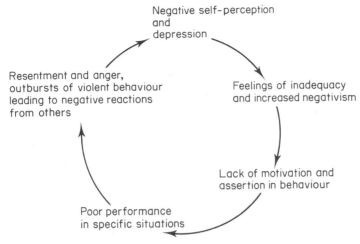

Figure 10.2.   Miranda: vicious circle of negative thoughts and aggressive behaviour

was needed, even with people not holding any particular authority, like librarians or shop assistants.

Valerie thought that Miranda would benefit from work on a one-to-one basis rather than inclusion in a group, for several reasons. First, Miranda's relationships with her immediate peer group were not easy and relaxed enough to foster a supportive atmosphere. There had been incidents in which she had become aggressive towards some of them after (she said) they had laughed at her. Eventually this kind of situation could be tackled in the group context, but Miranda was not ready for it at this stage. Secondly, Miranda needed to talk through some of her feelings of hurt and resentment towards others, and while this could be incorporated into an individual social skills programme, in a group it would have inhibited the process of learning. Thirdly, it would have been difficult to assemble a group with a stable membership in a setting where there was a constant succession of departures and new arrivals. Indeed, a major obstacle in trying to carry through any consistent programme to help people to work on their problems lies in the transient nature of the client group in settings like this, where clients and staff come together in what must appear an arbitrary and disjointed way. This lack of continuity is an unsatisfactory feature in a system ostensibly designed to help disturbed and unhappy children to find some sort of stability.

Helping to Build Self-confidence

Valerie and Miranda discussed the difficulties which had been highlighted and together they worked out a programme. The principal idea was that they would meet regularly to look at the situations and people that worried Miranda and try to work out ways of dealing with them more satisfactorily. They would have the use of a suitable room and a video camera and monitor. Valerie talked about the use of role-play to practise things we need to do and Miranda joined in with no difficulty. She found the practical, concrete approach of social skills training very easy to understand and to accept. As in any learning situation, understanding exactly what is being done and the reasons for it is an essential element.

As the programme started, a decision was taken to return Miranda to her home in the near future. This threw the work into temporary disarray. Valerie decided to make a virtue out of necessity and reconstructed the programme around similar but simpler and more immediate goals related to Miranda's ability to cope on leaving care. Video recordings show the sessions to have been discursive (chatty might be a better term), open-ended and flexible. Miranda helped by adjusting the camera angles and switching the monitor on and off, and was generally very much a participant. As the conversations proceeded, Valerie picked up points, challenged gently and gave supportive reinforcement to Miranda; her use of language was simple and clear, and she used humour to set Miranda at her ease and keep her relaxed.

Valerie was offering Miranda a model virtually throughout their sessions together and doing so in two different ways: first by modelling behaviour during the actual role-plays, but secondly also by her responses to Miranda in conversation as she discussed anxiety-provoking situations in a calm and logical manner. In this way she was able to outline and demonstrate the rational control of anxiety and the principles of problem-solving, and she persuaded Miranda to look objectively at situations where she thought people were laughing at her, helping her to see that she was misinterpreting their behaviour (for instance, the people concerned were already laughing before she had approached them). The opportunity to imitate a model with whom the client can identify and whose level of performance is attainable is a potent learning experience. Valerie supported this discussion by showing Miranda her own performance on video, demonstrating that there was nothing funny or odd about it. In general, Valerie shaped Miranda's behaviour towards a more assertive and autonomous expression of the girl's own wishes.

The TV monitor was used to play back role-plays illustrating discrete elements of behaviour and discussion developed quickly, with Valerie picking up aspects like eye contact, posture and voice production. Miranda's perception of her own appearance and behaviour soon started to change. For instance, in the early stages she referred to her voice as being "like a bloke's", but Valerie challenged this perception and used a replay from the monitor to demonstrate conclusively that Miranda's voice was in fact quite feminine, and that moreover if she were to slow down her rate of speech and take a little more trouble over pronunciation it would become even more so.

The actual role-plays used were very short and simple, geared to Miranda's immediate needs. Using video in this way allows enormous flexibility in the programme, with the client identifying the areas to be worked on. At some stages, Valerie also used role-reversal, so that Miranda could learn how it felt to be in the other person's shoes; this is a particularly useful device when video is not available.

In this piece of work, the learning of new behaviour was a real factor but is not in itself particularly remarkable. The reason for describing it here is the cognitive aspect of the work, the way in which Valerie helped Miranda to revise and restructure her perceptions of herself and her potential for interacting with others. Thinking through situations critically and analytically is vital, but on its own it is not sufficient to make change possible; it must be accompanied by the performance of linked, appropriate behaviour if progress is to be made. Valerie's evaluation of the work indicated that the desired gains had indeed been made. Certainly this is borne out by the evidence of the video recordings and Miranda herself was very pleased with the outcome, but, unfortunately, the circumstance of Miranda leaving care and returning home at the end of this short period made follow-up impossible.

SOCIAL SKILLS TRAINING WITH YOUNGER CHILDREN

In work with children, especially younger children, the principle of keeping to the client's pace assumes a particular importance; timing, sequencing and variety are all important if interest and enthusiasm are to be maintained. The limited attention span of primary-school children is proverbial, so training sessions need to be carefully timed on a "little and often" basis. Games can often be used to advantage, and, given a little ingenuity, some traditional children's games can be adapted for inclusion in this framework, whereas formality will bring sudden death to any attempt to work creatively with children. The best games are those that children can adapt and experiment with and in which peer group approval can be a feature. Young children are often not aware of each other's behaviour unless it impinges on them directly and do not provide each other with much reinforcement. Often the leader can help by modelling this. As in adult groups, appropriate praise and recognition need to be part of the ethos of group meetings.

Role-play can be seen as an extension of children's ordinary play, so it is not surprising that children often take to it more spontaneously than their elders; it is just a different form of "Let's pretend!". Games which centre on recognized social roles and functions are a favourite with many children, and policemen, doctors and nurses figure regularly in their games repertoire as a visit to any play-group will verify. Assuming some "official" role can often help a young client to show more assertiveness—or (as it is more usually expressed) to be less shy or timid. Simply being given the part of an imaginary policeman or teacher involves the right to speak up for yourself, and role-reversal lends itself well to this kind of work.

A distinction needs to be made between the use of play in social skills training and play therapy as practised in specialized settings such as child guidance clinics. Both kinds of approach stress that play has an intrinsic value in enabling children to learn, adapt, experiment and grow, and generally to cope with the demands life makes on them. In social skills training, however, it has the added function of developing awareness of behaviour and the way in which it may be changed and adapted. Clement and Milne (1967) compared a behavioural group which used token reinforcement with a play therapy group and a control group and found that the behavioural group was more effective in increasing the interaction between the children and in decreasing the level of problem behaviour. In the play therapy group there was an actual decrease in social play. Learning experiences need to be carefully structured because children may not discriminate in the way they learn through play and thus will repeat and adopt elements of behaviour which are undesirable or counterproductive. Teaching fine discrimination is not easy but it is essential for real progress. To appreciate and gain control over our behaviour we need both good powers of discrimination (the ability, for instance, to distinguish between situations calling for different responses) and the opportunity to receive accurate feedback.

Several writers have dealt with the use of play to pinpoint pieces of behaviour, notably Rose (1972), who sees the function of play in social skills training primarily in terms of its potential as a vehicle for change. The attractiveness of the group setting for participants must not be allowed to detract from the central purpose of the group, which is to enhance social skills. Rose comments that: "High group attraction is a two-edged sword: if the group is too attractive, members may spend most of their energy maintaining it and reinforcing each other's minimal accomplishments. Activities which give the group recognition become more highly valued than increasing needed social skills". When a group is newly formed priority will usually be given to fostering cohesion and interaction, but as the work proceeds the task of learning new behaviour should soon start to take precedence. Such a group is in fact displaying the classic developmental stages of forming, storming, norming and performing.

The care which may have to go into these early stages of the work with young children is well illustrated by the care which Jim, a young worker in a small group home for some quite disturbed children, put into the formation of a group to work on a number of behavioural problems. The setting was a particularly difficult one in that many of the children showed not only disturbance in their behaviour but also resentment at being in the home at all. Initially Jim moved the group outside the children's home for weekly meetings and introduced the video system to the children, encouraging them to help in setting it up and operating it. The first four meetings were a mix of play and discussion, with the children becoming used to the video and to another staff member who was joining them to help run the group. At this stage Jim was concentrating primarily on relationship building and on familiarizing the children with the idea of observing themselves on video, thereby building up their confidence and trust in the workers. Discussion about their everyday lives was encouraged, and the children were involved in their own assessment by the use of both video and self-report. This rather tentative and exploratory approach reflected Jim's awareness of the children's living environment and the feelings they might have about it. He concentrated initially on the formation and cohesion of the group, leaving it to a later stage to shift the emphasis on to the learning tasks. His approach displays the necessary flexibility but he never lost sight of the longer-term learning objectives. In any case, the early meetings contributed greatly to the thoroughness of the assessment, which it was possible in this way to make a genuinely shared enterprise despite the youth of those concerned.

SOCIAL CONTROL OR SOCIAL ACCEPTABILITY?

This chapter began with a consideration of the issue of social control as it is raised by this approach. There should, however, be no ethical problem involved in helping clients to modify behaviour which impedes their development. Nobody will be seen as socially skilled who, though good at communicating with others, nevertheless displays some form of behaviour which prevents him or her from forming and maintaining good social relationships. On occasions such maladaptive behaviour can not only antagonize staff in institutions but also involve other problems for the client concerned, both within the institution and outside it.

One example of such a situation is the work done by Karen, a housemother in a children's home where Paul, a large 15-year-old boy with learning difficulties, frequently antagonized or upset female staff members. Karen became aware that there was a problem here from the acrimonious comments of her colleagues about the boy, and especially about his habit of standing very close to them in a way which made them feel very uncomfortable. Karen carried out some observations herself, concluding that her colleagues' complaints had a basis in reality, and decided to try to

help both Paul and her colleagues through a social skills programme. A complicating factor was the way staff responded when
they felt Paul was invading their personal space. Karen suspected
that their expression of anxiety and apprehension was actually
reinforcing Paul's behaviour.

Karen motivated Paul to work on this behaviour by discussing with
him the probable future consequences if it were to continue. At the
same time she talked to other staff about the programme she had in
mind in order to gain their cooperation; she was generally successful in securing their support, although one or two of them expressed
doubts. The programme which Karen worked out included using
pictures of people talking together to help improve Paul's ability to
discriminate between different kinds of situation, as well as rehearsal in role-plays with token reinforcement. Following this programme Paul showed considerable improvement in the way he
approached staff within the establishment, though there is no information on whether his behaviour changed outside the home as
well.

Children take very readily to social skills training. Learning by doing
is a familiar experience to them and learning in groups, experimenting and testing out are part of their everyday life. They do not view
training sessions as an arbitrary imposition by adults of some alien
code of values or behaviour but rather as an opportunity to try out
new kinds of activity in a secure, non-threatening setting. As Rose
(1972) comments:

> In most instances children view modeling and rehearsal pro-
> cedures as enjoyable diversions while they are changing their
> behavior. For the therapist however, modeling and rehearsal
> procedures are central to the whole treatment process.

For children, as for adults, effective change may require not merely
behavioural learning but an improved way of understanding oneself
and one's situation, a more positive view of the self and an enhanced
capacity for problem-solving. Meichenbaum (1977) cites a large
number of studies which demonstrate the particular effectiveness in
working with children of a combination of operant learning (the use
of rewards) and self-instruction, the use of language "to alter the
child's thinking style on the one hand, and on the other his overt
behavior". By the use of this approach children, far from being

reduced to uniformity and compliance, can achieve more satisfaction in their interaction with others and a more positive image of themselves and their ability to meet the challenges which life will offer them.

CHAPTER 11   Work with physically handicapped clients

This chapter will describe in some detail two pieces of work with physically handicapped clients, one with blind and partially sighted children and the other with profoundly deaf young men. Here, the handicaps concerned are so substantial that it is more appropriate to discuss the work in this context than in the context of the age group of the clients concerned; it is quite plainly the nature of the handicap which requires the work to take the direction that it does and which suggests to the workers concerned (both with considerable experience with the client group) the ways in which they need to modify and adapt the basic method of social skills training to take account of the circumstances and capacities of their clients. The term "handicap" is used in preference to "disability" to indicate "the disadvantage or restriction of activity caused by disability". Indeed, it has a more positive connotation to it, in that "disability" stresses impotence, the inability to do what others do, whereas "handicap" implies that these things can be done, albeit with some difficulty. Undesirable though it is to label individuals as members of a category, the real disadvantages and restrictions suffered by handicapped people must be recognized. Implicit in that very recognition is the desire to help them improve their situation and lessen their disadvantages.

There are two further general points to be made. First, that the families of disabled people can actually *increase* the degree of handicap by overprotection and oversolicitous behaviour, and may need to draw back a little to allow the individual to develop to the full. This is really a special case of something which happens in many, perhaps most families, especially where the children are seen as particularly vulnerable. Secondly, practitioners with a specific client group recognize that the disability affecting that group rarely occurs in isolation, being usually accompanied by others either coinciding with it or arising in consequence. The clients whose progress is charted in this chapter have all encountered additional problems and these have resulted in varying degrees of multiple handicap.

CHILDREN WITH VISUAL HANDICAPS

Nowhere are the problems surrounding a primary disability more discernible than in the case of a visually handicapped child, and they can be compounded by the impact of the condition itself on workers who come new to it. What image could be more emotive than that of a blind child? No client is more likely to appeal to our protective instincts. The three examples of work which follow come from a school for visually handicapped children which has a residential facility for weekly boarding by children whose homes are too distant for them to attend as day pupils. The change from termly to weekly boarding a few years ago, together with increased stress on family involvement in the child's progress at the school, has helped to maintain family bonds while continuing to offer a counter to parental overprotectiveness, but the system still has drawbacks.

Some years before the publication of the Warnock Report (1978) advocated the integration of handicapped children into mainstream education, the National Federation of the Blind was already commenting that because the schools attended by a majority of visually handicapped children were segregated, the children were being deprived within the schools of a fundamental element in their education, namely the opportunity to know, understand and work with their unhandicapped peers. A handicapped person has to learn to live in the world of the unhandicapped, they argued, and the prolonged segregation of children can artificially retard this process and intensify the problem. Moves to offset the effects of a segregated school by integrating children into local activities such as Brownie Guides and Cub Scouts do not entirely counteract this negative effect.

The need to provide opportunities for children to learn mastery over their environment is highlighted by Elizabeth Chapman (1978):

> Difficulties in managing routine social skills are likely to have been exacerbated if the visually handicapped child has been discouraged from doing things for himself at home, or has spent years in an institutional atmosphere where many of his daily needs are catered for without effort or physical contribution from him.

The Warnock Report makes a number of similar points, notably children's need to learn discrimination between behavioural expectations and norms in different situations and their need to experience a variety of social situations where learning is interesting and rewarding.

The visually handicapped child's restricted experience in the first years of life results in a developmental lag which calls for a planned remedial input. She or he needs, for instance, some substitute for the visual imitation of the sighted child, who learns in a casual way to engage in a wide variety of activity such as walking, speech, postural and gestural movements and general expressive behaviour. The child sees and imitates many of these behaviours going on around and takes them into her or his own repertoire by imitation and repetition. A lot of basic but quite complex procedures such as eating and dressing are not so much taught as copied, and the same applies to many of the skills involved in interaction and communication. The visually handicapped child, denied to a large extent these possibilities of learning through imitation, needs an enriched environment to compensate for their absence. Touch and hearing cues, together with verbal and physical prompting and coaching, can be used to increase the child's ability to discriminate. Specific experiences have to be provided and structured into a coherent programme; the child needs to learn about situations in their *totality* rather than in a fragmented, disjointed manner, and learning by *doing* will help to compensate for the reduced stimulation received from the environment. Concentration on developing skills and achieving mastery over the environment will help the child to develop at the same time an improved image of the self as a potentially competent person.

Many visually handicapped children look odd; their gestures seem strange and clumsy, for easy and purposeful movement is not achieved in virtual isolation. Denied the opportunity to take part in many physical activities by overprotective parents, they lose the chance to experiment on their environment, and a structured sequence of movement training can be provided in the form of play activities to counteract this, using enhanced body movements and with continuous feedback to reinforce progress and to motivate and shape future behaviour. Visually handicapped children seem to display more speech peculiarities than other children, so may need extra guidance in this area too. Because they cannot use visual observation to provide associations, they very often produce non-sense words which are then retained in their vocabulary (rather than disappearing spontaneously, as with most children). "Verbalism" of this kind is thus a product of the child's impoverished first-hand experiences rather than of any emotional disorder.

Staff working with children in a setting of this kind have to take account of these behaviours and the factors which produce and maintain them, and to bear constantly in mind the child's lack of sight in devising methods of coaching and modelling which will provide some compensation for it.

Assessing Performance and Needs

Because the child operates in several environments, information needs to be gathered from each of them, viz:

(a) at home (self-report, parents, social worker, mobility officer, others)
(b) school (self-report, staff, peers)
(c) outside environment (ditto, plus interested outsider)

Considerable differences are often found between the way the child performs in these different environments: for instance, a child who is apparently unable to do something at home may manage it without difficulty at school. Even within the school there may be discrepancies in performance, so that children who can tie their shoe-laces in the classroom have the job done for them by residential staff.

Various kinds of information are needed in order to assess a child's current level of development and ability. A thorough medical and ophthalmic investigation is necessary, together with a consideration of intellectual and emotional development; language acquisition requires particular attention. Sometimes visual defects are accompanied by disturbances in motor control, usually readily discernible, and these too must be noted. These specialist findings must be integrated with observations by care staff and teachers within the establishment; the expressed wishes and concerns of the child and the parents are also a vital factor. Where a child goes outside the school for some social activities, the views of outsiders can also be helpful. Such information must, of course, be interpreted in the light of the person making the observations and the setting in which they took place.

Divergence between the norms of home and of school and difference in expectations of the child are also very important. Children need to become aware of the differences between the two and develop their capacity to discriminate between what is expected of them. This is a crucial part of their learning, and if they have any problems around this they need to be able to discuss them with staff and to feel that the home environment is neither any better nor any worse than the school, just different. Sometimes the parents' help can be enlisted in assessing the child's performance at home and this not only makes the assessment more complete but also can offer an opportunity to make a real contribution to their child's progress. Actually working with the families can also be a great asset in social skills training.

The three programmes to be described here were carried out by Hazel, a senior housemother in the residential unit attached to a special school, who had a good existing relationship with the children concerned and also had access to full assessments of the type described above. Hence she did not need to carry out an exhaustive assessment of her own, merely supplementing the material with one or two specific observations.

Programme for an Eight-year-old Girl: Identifying Problems and Objectives

Debbie was a girl of eight, previously assessed as educationally backward, with limited residual vision and that in one eye only. She had a difficult home life, with parents who were discouraged and preoccupied by their own problems, and two other children of the family were in residential schools. Debbie's mother did maintain contact, however, visiting once a term and phoning twice a week. Her father had been unemployed for some years and had a drink problem. Both parents did their best to cooperate with their local social worker, who gave them a lot of support.

The overall aim of the programme with Debbie was to teach her to deliver a message in an appropriate manner. Assessment indicated a number of problem factors which interfered with her ability to communicate: posture, with head held to one side and lowered; eye contact, which was minimal, with her eyes cast down; verbal competence, with indistinct, mumbling speech which was very quiet with adults but loud with other children and with very limited vocabulary and comprehension; and general manner of approach, which was often inappropriate to the circumstances. These difficulties were thought to be caused by the visual handicap itself, by inappropriate parental modelling, by a lack of opportunity to explore a variety of social situations and by her limited learning capacity and comprehension. The problems thus identified suggested the following as desirable and possible objectives for change:

- Correction of posture, holding up her head and facing the other person
- Improved eye contact to approximate to more usual patterns
- Oral changes, with clearer speech, appropriate volume and pitch
- Manner of approach, discriminating between formal and informal settings

Setting up the Programme

Hazel discussed Debbie's problems in fairly general terms with other staff members, explaining social skills training methods and the need for structured programmes which involved coaching, modelling, repeated practice and reinforcement contingent on successful performance. As with the other children she was working with, she also discussed the subject with the client herself, encouraging her to talk about her own needs and to participate in a programme which was intended to be not only useful but also interesting—in fact, fun. Some discussion with other children as well ensured that they were fully aware of what was going forward and the reasons for it so as to elicit their cooperation.

A precise situation was then identified to work on. This was to be taking a message to a named teacher in the classroom, and was broken down into discrete steps, as follows:

1. Locate correct classroom

2. Knock on door
3. Wait for response
4. Enter classroom
5. Either approach teacher direct or ask "Is Mr Pring here?"
6. Wait if teacher is occupied
7. Give appropriate greeting "Hello, Mr Pring" and await response
8. Identify the sender of the message: "Miss Thomas said . . ."
9. Repeat text of message
10. Wait for reply or question, if any
11. Give appropriate closure: "Thank you; goodbye"
12. Leave classroom

The significant pieces of verbal behaviour involved in this sequence were: opening and closing conversations, asking and answering questions, and clear, sufficiently loud speech with accurate content. The non-verbal behaviour involved comprised mobility skill (locating the classroom), posture and gait, approach and proximity, and finally eye contact. The programme took the form of a series of individual sessions with Debbie, working on elements like eye contact and proximity, using modelling and physical prompts as well as verbal prompts and shaping. The importance and value of touch for blind people means that in programmes like this they need actually to feel the extent of the space between themselves and others in order to appreciate it, and similarly to feel carefully people's faces, both other people's and their own, in order to recognize what they are conveying by their facial expression and how they might change it according to what they are trying to communicate.

Working with Debbie in a Group; Evaluating the Progress Made

After the individual sessions, Hazel went on to a series of five group sessions with other children who could participate and help, themselves learning at the same time. In the first session she made a great deal of use of modelling, as well as coaching and rehearsal, and delivered a "message" to each member of the group in turn, then letting them practise the same task with each other in pairs. Debbie herself was cued in by using questions to remind her of the elements: who are you taking the message to? where will he be? what is the message? She was reinforced throughout for her improving performance and the rest of the group were shaped up to provide encouragement by praise for their helpfulness.

Subsequent sessions followed a similar pattern, each one beginning with a recap of the previous weeks' learning. In session two Hazel modelled discrimination in the way a message is delivered, showing the different elements involved in giving a message to a staff member rather than to another blind child, and in the third she developed the interchange to make it more complicated by including the need to answer questions. For instance, a staff member receiving the message that Jennie is ill might ask: "What is the matter with her?" or "When will she be back?". In session four she varied the approach by modelling some undesirable behaviour, such as whispering or standing too close, and invited the children to criticize her performance and then to do it better themselves. This is a very useful technique for helping people to improve their discrimination and it usually works particularly well, since it almost always raises a laugh and hence helps to decrease any anxieties group members may be feeling. The final session gave an opportunity for questions and answers as well as developing the situations played so as to call for a wider range of responses.

Programme with a Boy of Nine on Use of Telephone

This was a much less complex programme with nine-year-old John, who had very limited residual vision (1/60 and 3/60) and who wanted to be able to speak to his parents on the telephone during the week. It consisted of two sessions per week, lasting between 10 and 20 minutes, for about a month. The programme started with practise at dialling and speaking, using a Playphone. John had difficulty with the sequencing of the actions required, for instance he would dial before lifting the receiver. Visual prompts were, of course, out of the question and modelling was only of limited use, so he was coached and guided by whispered prompts and a light touch on his arm. He also practised answering the phone by saying "Hullo, this is John. Can I help you?". In the three sessions following the initial one he used the junior house-phone for practice, learned to discriminate between house calls and outside ones, and conducted conversations of increasing length. Next, after another rehearsal with the Playphone, he went on to call the school from an outside coin-operated box. This requires a complicated sequence of actions, and despite the rehearsal he still required physical prompts to remind him of it and some help in inserting the money in the slot. It was only after several rehearsals that he could feel sure of remembering the right things to say. After some more practise with local calls the programme ended with John making a long-distance call to his parents. Certainly no additional reinforcement was required at this stage, and indeed John was so highly motivated to learn this new skill, difficult though he found it, that little reinforcement was necessary. There was one final difficulty in that John could not read the long-distance codes in the usual print, but Hazel was able to obtain a large-print version for his continuing use.

Attractive and satisfying though this programme was for John, it was important for him to have the opportunity for continued practice or the gains might have been lost. The reader may wonder: what is it about this activity of teaching a child to use the telephone that makes it social skills training rather than just another piece of learning? The overall aim has an evident social component, in that its achievement will foster communication between parents and child, but another essential feature, which distinguishes it from the everyday learning processes which occur in every child's development, is the method by which the learning is made possible, the careful structuring of a programme consisting of graded tasks through which the child is enabled to progress despite a constellation of impeding factors. A training programme of this kind has to be carefully designed to counter each of these specific impediments.

Social Skills and Mobility: Training Programme with a Boy of 10

Social skills training for 10-year-old Matthew was linked to his general mobility training. This, of course, is always important for visually handicapped children, and Matthew presented special problems in that he would often run about in a very wild, uncontrolled way; he was also described as rude and uncooperative in certain situations. He was very keen, however, to work towards an outing to the city centre and this was established as the goal of the programme: Matthew was to take responsibility for ordering a meal in a restaurant and was to be given the money to pay for it.

The early stages of the programme involved crossing safely first the school drive, then a minor road and finally a busy main road, then making purchases in the local small shop. Matthew learned next how to locate the bus stop and to buy tickets, and finally progressed to the anticipated excursion with Hazel to the city centre. As with the previous programmes, it was important to structure the learning in successive stages and to consolidate and build on the behaviour which had been learned early on. The mobility officer was able to follow up the programme with a similar one based on Matthew's home, a particularly useful device since parents are often incredulous when told of the new things their child has learned to do. It seems too good to be true.

General Features of Work with the Blind Children

The main techniques used were prompting (with progressive fading of the prompts), shaping and rehearsal. Physical prompts were used a lot, with maximum help being given in the early stages, the worker using her own hands to guide those of the child to carry out the tasks. Initially she would work very close to the child, guiding and turning the head in the required direction. She also used beckoning and pointing where there was sufficient sight, but quietly spoken or whispered prompts necessarily played an important part in the work.

The most frequently used methods of reinforcement were social, in the form of praise and encouragement from the worker herself and in Debbie's case from other children and other staff members; with Matthew, food and drink were used as well. Using a mix of reinforcers rather than a single method, and above all selecting an overall objective which the children were highly motivated to achieve (John and Matthew), helped to make the programmes more attractive and effective. It is, of course, always important that reinforcement is contingent upon learning: that is, that it is only given for a performance at least as good as the preceding one. On one occasion John made a mistake in sequencing his actions in making a phone call; it would have been confusing to give any reinforcement at this point. Initially every step in the programmes was rewarded, with the reinforcement fading to intermittent and being eventually discontinued. The fact that the new behaviour learned offered the children some intrinsic satisfaction ensured, however, that the progress made would not be lost.

DEAFNESS: WORK WITH HEARING-IMPAIRED YOUNG MEN

The communication problems experienced by deaf and partially deaf people require no stressing here, indeed they are familiar to most people, whether specialists or not. What is worth noting, however, is that, unlike a blind child, a deaf young man, particularly one who gesticulates and speaks incoherently, is not an obvious candidate for sympathy. Hence, social skills have a particular significance for him, especially as regards ways of approaching strangers who may be unfamiliar with his handicap. The project which is described in the rest of this chapter was planned and carried out in a residential home which provides social and vocational training for about 30 profoundly prelingually deaf young men between the ages of 16 and 22, most of whom are multiply handicapped, having only partial sight, some form of spasticity, a cleft palate or some other physical impairment in addition to their deafness. Many of the trainees have encountered difficulties in special schools for deaf children, perhaps having actually been expelled. Some have come to the home because of difficulties with their families, while others have been referred after contact with the police and the courts or from psychiatric units. Many of them have a long history of institutional care.

The first four weeks at the centre are spent in assessing the new arrival's suitability for the various forms of training on offer. A trainee will circulate round the trade courses during this period and each instructor, together with the youth's key-worker, will prepare a report on his behaviour and progress. The centre uses a standard Gunzberg (target-type) Personal Assessment Chart, specially modified for use with the deaf. During the usual two and a half years' stay at least three case conferences are held on each individual trainee.

Setting up a Project in the Residential Training Centre

Tom, an instructor at the centre, wanted to set up a social skills project, but he was aware of a number of constraints. First, the trainees are limited by their minute vocabulary of signed language —some 200–500 words as compared with the average vocabulary of some 2000 words displayed by the five-year-old starting school. Secondly, a delayed cognitive and moral development may cause difficulties in communicating about abstract qualities or moral issues. Thirdly, while there is considerable variation in the intelligence levels of the trainees, some have specific additional problems in this area and this, together with their limited vocabulary and powers of expression, makes discussion difficult. Fourthly, some trainees suffer from varying degrees and types of mental instability, in particular from a form of autism characterized by bizarre behaviour. Lastly, the worker felt somewhat uneasy about the ethical basis for work in which he would have to anticipate decisions or sometimes even take them on behalf of his clients. These considerations inevitably limit any work to be attempted with the client group, and the possibility of working effectively in groups is moreover circumscribed by the difficulty one member will have in understanding anything not addressed directly to him and by the need to give extra attention to the aggressive and noisy group member, possibly at the expense of the quiet and introverted.

Assessing a Deaf Young Man for Social Skills Training

The work described was carried out with Andy, a young man of 20, partly on an individual basis but in the context of similar work with a group of similar clients. Tom had been struck by the way in which Andy would antagonize people (mainly staff members) by his noisy, disruptive behaviour and he wanted to find out how Andy saw himself and how he was perceived by his peers, as well as how staff viewed him. He therefore devised a test to establish this, in the form of a simple bipolar grid, which he tested out on his own children in order to ensure that it was readily comprehensible; in fact he had started with a five-point scale but had to abandon this as too complicated for his purpose. The questions related to such factors as whether Andy saw himself as quiet or noisy, happy or miserable, selfish or unselfish, and so on. The findings which emerged showed the various respondents as in agreement on some particulars but as diverging on others: thus staff members described Andy as "selfish" and "not shy", whereas he saw himself as "unselfish" and "shy", a perception with which his fellow trainees agreed. On the other hand, staff saw Andy as "noisy" rather than quiet and here other trainees agreed with the staff view rather than sharing Andy's that he was "quiet".

Bearing these discrepancies in mind, Tom selected a piece of behaviour identified as causing problems both for staff and for Andy himself. It is worth noting that again, as with much of the work described in this book, the client in question was enabled to grasp the nature of his problem and was motivated to work on resolving it by the classic techniques of individual counselling, reflection, clarification and challenge, together with information and explanation of what could be done to help. The problem identified for work was, then, Andy's existing method of opening a conversation, interrupting people who were already talking or engaged on a task in a noisy, intrusive manner. The conditions were specified more precisely as follows:

- Where? Especially at the training centre, but also to some extent outside.
- When? Particularly on entering a room, when excited or when there was an audience.
- With whom? Authority figures and other hearing people known to him, also to a lesser extent with peers.
- With what outcome? Andy usually received attention and the problem behaviour was thereby reinforced. Others, however, became frustrated and annoyed, and this led to confrontations which could escalate into aggression and even violence.
- Why? It appeared that there had been faulty learning of behaviour in the past; there was also sporadic reinforcement from the peer group. Moreover, like many deaf youngsters, Andy, being insensitive to noise himself, did not realize its effect on hearing people. It is also possible that he was overcompensating for the shyness which he saw in himself but others failed to perceive.

The Programme—Learning Skills of Self-Presentation

The reinforcers were to be praised, especially in front of peers; being accorded positions of responsibility, status and power in the centre; and excursions for shopping and ice-skating, or invitations to family homes. This is a notably wide array of rewards as compared with programmes with some other client groups—people like Andy, who have experienced a great deal of failure and discouragement in the past, may often need the extra boost to their motivation and persistence which such a complex system of reinforcers can offer. Most of the actual work was performed in the context of the more general social training which Tom was carrying out with his usual group, and which included some topics brought up by group members themselves. Hence they were already familiar with the ideas and some of the methods involved and well motivated to provide support and encouragement.

In session one, Andy was sent from his usual working group to the training group with a simple message and his arrival and manner of delivering the message recorded on video. This immediately gave something concrete to work on, so that Andy's willingness to participate could be confirmed; had Andy been at all reluctant to join the group and to work with them, Tom would have offered him the option at this point of continuing on an individual basis. In the event, however, Andy welcomed the opportunity to become part of the group, in which there were several members he already knew quite well and looked up to. On the rerun of the video Andy had little difficulty in seeing the deficiencies in his behaviour and with a little coaching he was able to give a markedly improved performance. The group, too, were enthusiastic about Andy's joining them and readily contributed ideas of their own towards the coaching. While this initial session was clearly very successful, Tom commented afterwards that he might with advantage have spent more time in making Andy feel at home in the group and on praising him for improvements in his performance. At this stage little reinforcement from the worker other than praise was required, since Andy responded very well to the increased attention and approval he was receiving from his peers. At the end of the last video sequence Andy finished by signing to the other group members: "I want all of you to try to help me learn".

The second session was prefaced by some individual work with Andy in which Tom used what he had learned from his assessment tool (the bipolar grid) to show Andy some of the differences between the way he saw himself and the way staff saw him. They then went on to recall together the boisterous way he had entered the group the previous week and discussed how this might lead other people to see him as "noisy" and how he had learned to do it better.

Further sessions then continued with the group, now including Andy and giving him a certain amount of prominence, working on commonplace situations derived from recent experience. On one occasion a female staff member was invited to join the group, since it was women staff in particular who had complained about noisy interruptions by Andy (among others). On another, Andy was given some help and reassurance over his anxiety about a new set of false teeth which he had just acquired and which he was afraid might have a bad effect on his appearance and the general impression he made; the video was a great help with this. The accent throughout the programme was on flexibility and on working with the situations of most concern to the trainees at any particular time.

During the programme Tom found he had to do considerable work with his colleagues in order to ensure that Andy was reinforced outside the group for any improvements in behaviour, since it was clear that in the past Andy had been rewarded for inappropriate behaviour by being accorded extra attention. Initially, Tom was disappointed to find that when Andy entered a room quietly and correctly, instead of bursting in noisily as had been his habit, he was all but ignored. After this incident Tom took great care to ensure that his colleagues were sufficiently in sympathy with the programme that the gains made would be maintained and consolidated.

General Comments

This project highlights a number of points. First, for deaf people communication is a natural and obvious problem area and any difficulties they encounter are enormously magnified. Hence, the difference between an unwelcome interruption and an acceptable, everyday manner of entering a situation and embarking on a conversation is a frequent issue which can be tackled productively by social skills training. Again, because deaf people rely so heavily on visual information, video can be a tremendous help to them. Another factor, which reflects the stage of development of the clients (late adolescence) as well as the handicap, was Tom's approach to assessment, which involved the views of peers as well as Andy's own judgement. In Tom's opinion, it was unlikely that Andy would have accepted some of the perceptions which staff members had of him had they not been supported by those of his peers. Colleagues, too, have to be involved in the work in order to ensure a successful outcome, but it is one of the advantages of practising this approach in a group care setting that securing collaboration of this kind is indeed a possibility. For the newly learned behaviour to be further generalized, thought would need to be given to how a client like Andy might ensure that he could gain attention politely and pleasantly in places where he was known less well, such as local shops.

Social skills work with handicapped people has its own peculiar difficulties, but a worker who knows the client group well and has developed the ability to communicate with them and help them will find this a very useful and creative addition to the repertoire of helping methods available to him. Sensory handicaps, deafness perhaps most of all, tend to cut people off from the rest of humanity, so that any method of helping them to develop and improve their skills of communication and interaction has something very special and precious to offer them.

CHAPTER 12   Social skills and mental handicap

Approaching this area of work immediately raises a question of terminology. The term "mental handicap" which has been in use in Britain until recently is now being replaced in many contexts by "learning disability" or "learning difficulties" as these expressions are seen as being less stigmatizing. Unfortunately they are also less comprehensible, and the latter in particular is readily confused with educational problems such as dyslexia. Such a term is so wide and imprecise that it could be applied to groups of people to whom the mental handicap services have no conceivable relevance. People like the physically handicapped clients whose progress was described in the last chapter have severe and manifest learning difficulties quite irrespective of their intellectual capacities, so there is a clear need for a term which indicates the presence of an additional problem related to intelligence. In general, then, we are using the older term "mental handicap", which, though criticized by some, at least has the advantage that it is understood by all, both in North America and elsewhere in Europe ("handicap" is also the French term, for instance). It is, after all, the function of language to enlighten, not to mystify.

The World Health Organisation in its classification of diseases and disabilities uses the term "mental retardation" (also current in America) and establishes four categories of profound, severe, moderate and mild mental retardation, on the basis of IQ but with a brief reference to the individual's capacity to respond to training and acquire skills. The document also identifies a sequence: disease —impairment—disability—handicap. Here the notion of handicap is seen as introducing a new element, that of the social consequences of the condition. The Mental Health Act of 1959 already adopted a somewhat different approach to definition, identifying the individual's ability to cope with the demands of everyday life as the criterion for the help or care that person should be given rather than any objective, once-for-all system of measurement and assessment.

The concept of "skilled performance" in a variety of contexts is another way of assessing an individual's potential, and social skills training after an assessment of this kind will offer an optimistic and realistic method of enhancing the person's ability to cope and survive in the environment. The initial level of performance must never be assumed to be a permanent, fixed limit, but rather a threshold or springboard to further progress and development. This way of thinking is characteristic of the social skills approach, which emphasizes what a person can actually do now and may learn to do, given suitable opportunities, rather than presuming or establishing an intellectual ceiling. Clearly, intellectual endowment is a relevant factor when potential is being assessed, but it is often not the most important, and certainly not the most helpful consideration. Mentally handicapped people living in large institutions or in over-protective families have always, moreover, tended to underperform, and it is only recently that we have realized how much unactivated capacity has been lying dormant as more stress has been placed on individual needs and choices and on self-responsibility and self-advocacy.

It is, in fact, often quite possible to offer social skills training in a group which includes one or two mentally handicapped people among its members, like the group whose operation was described in Chapter 8. Where the handicap is more severe a more specialized group is usually appropriate and remarkably encouraging results have been achieved even with clients whose problems include very limited speech, given the participation of committed staff, an adequate ratio of helpers to clients and a good knowledge of the method. In fact, the knowledge and interpersonal skills required of the worker who wishes to set up a programme are not essentially different from those developed in the normal course of face-to-face work with the same clients. The programmes which will be described were carried out in two day centres in different counties by students nearing the end of in-service professional training, so that in learning to practise social skills training as a method of helping they were building on considerable experience and knowledge about the client group and the agency as well as on the work done in the area of interpersonal skills at earlier stages of their course.

A "GETTING TO KNOW YOU" PROGRAMME IN A DAY CENTRE

In the first project Frank, an instructor in a day centre, spent some time discussing with a group of trainees what kinds of social situations made them feel worried and inhibited. Four of them, young men with mild to moderate handicap and ranging in age from the late teens to the early thirties, were keen to take part in a group which would work on these situations. These young men had already been members of a group providing social training of a more general kind, and so were used to each other and to the idea of working in a group. The main subject of concern for these clients was the difficulty they experienced in forming and developing relationships with other people outside the centre, and the tasks the group would work on were selected by the clients themselves to exemplify this difficulty. Frank used several checklists which group members completed to highlight the kind of difficulties they were encountering and to suggest ways of overcoming them. The main list used for assessment comprised 15 items, quite specific situations ranging from solitary activities like walking down the street to entering and mixing with differently constituted groups in various settings; members scored it on a five-point scale, from "no difficulty at all" to "avoid if possible". While this may sound quite a complicated undertaking for people with learning difficulties, the group members in fact had no great difficulty in completing it, probably because the situations listed were so clearly and specifically stated. There was a general tendency to score high on meeting people for the first time, being with older people, approaching people and making the first move in a piece of interaction, but one group member, Ralph, emerged as less inhibited than other group members. Frank paid attention here, as throughout the programme, to maintaining the confidence of the group members and therefore chose to start and finish the checklist with neutral items such as walking down the street and talking to one's pet which he was sure would arouse no anxiety. Hence the operation of completing the checklist could start and conclude on a positive note.

Frank devised two more checklists to use as they went on, the first concerning voice production and covering six items: volume, tone, pitch, clarity, pace and speech disturbance, with rating on a three-point scale—"Volume: too quiet/normal/too loud" for instance. The second related to non-verbal behaviour, for instance "Proximity: too distant/normal/too close" and "Eye contact: too much avoidance/normal/stares". The other items were physical appearance, facial expressions, gestures and posture.

The programme comprised six sessions, using both video and audio-tapes to monitor the work and provide feedback to the members on their progress. Apart from its effectiveness as a tool in the learning, the video once more demonstrated how useful it can be as a rein-forcer in its own right, provoking interest and excitement through the enjoyment members derived from it. Whenever video is used it is likely to be an excellent policy to involve clients in actually operating it, since familiarity soon overcomes any initial anxieties and generates positive feelings of competence and mastery which in general they experience all too rarely. Engaging and involving members as actively as possible in the work of the group has a tremendous payoff in terms of stimulating interest and maintaining motivation, and it generally demystifies the helping process in a way that is particularly appropriate to this approach.

In addition to involving the group members in the operation of the sessions, Frank sought from the outset to secure the support of colleagues and brought one member of the staff both to help him to monitor and evaluate the sessions and to take part in some of the role-plays. One of us (John) also took part in one of the later sessions as a suitable "stranger" for members to meet.

Course of the Programme

The first session began with Frank explaining what the programme would involve and the methods which would be used. The group then completed the assessment checklist, from which they identified and then discussed the problem situations they would hope to work on. In session two, the group used the other checklists and con-centrated on voice production and also on posture and eye contact. Frank gave the whole group an opening line which could be used to start a conversation and then began himself by role-playing it with his co-worker. After watching the leaders modelling the inter-change two or three times (with minor variations to demonstrate that there is not one single right way to do it) the members took turns in role-playing it, with a tape-recorder to monitor the sequences. These short exchanges were repeated several times to enable group members to approximate to the modelled interchange, with Frank focusing on the volume, pitch, clarity and pace of speech and reinforcing any progress made, however small, by generous praise. Some attention was also given to posture, proximity and eye contact. Video was introduced for the first time in the third session and a sequence from the previous week's work was demonstrated by Frank and a group member and then played out by all the members in turn, with Frank recording aspects of the performances on the checklist as well as using video playback.

In session four, specific situations were contributed by group members and some more extensive role-plays were carried out based on the problems the members had brought. One of these was a very difficult situation in which the member concerned had actually assaulted an instructor at the centre. He had been told to go to the canteen by the instructor in a rather peremptory manner, whereupon he got into an argument with him which ended in his striking the staff member. Frank suggested that they might find it helpful to role-play this situation reversing the roles; in this way he modelled a more appropriate response despite the best efforts of the young man, in the role of instructor, to antagonize him. Of course, the roles had then to be reversed again and the scene replayed, with the level of provocation offered being very low at first but successively increasing. Another situation was a job interview which was in prospect for another member. This Frank broke up into several discrete, manageable steps and rehearsed the client through them, before inviting John (as tutor visiting the project) to play the part as the stranger conducting the interview. In both of these pieces of work short sequences were videoed, with coaching, modelling and reinforcement interspersed with replays which illustrated the progress being made and could also be used to make general points applicable to the performance of all the group members. Now that they were working not on problems shared by all the members but on aspects of special concern to one individual it was particularly important to encourage other members to participate by showing interest and approval; peer group approval of this kind is a most potent reinforcer, as was very apparent here. However, it frequently has to be worked at; often the approval which people so much appreciate receiving is something they themselves very seldom express. Thus, the idea that you have to "give to get" may need to be deliberately cultivated in groups of this kind, where there may well be members who, in their earlier lives, have lacked approval and encouragement from those around them and consequently express very little themselves. Hence they continue to receive little approval and the vicious circle is complete.

Frank used the fifth meeting of the group to try to generalize some of the behaviour which had been learned and they all went out to a local coffee bar where members could order the various items they wanted: reinforcement as well as generalization! Frank monitored their behaviour, paying special attention to voice quality and non-verbal behaviour, and there was some time afterwards for feedback and discussion of this. The final session was used for evaluation of the sequence, employing an audiotape to record members' opinions and feelings about what the programme had achieved. They also completed a second model of the original assessment checklist to see if they felt differently about the problem situations which figured on them. While Frank had been able to note objectively progress which had been achieved in particular respects, it was equally important that the members' own subjective views of their social competence should show a positive change, since confidence building and improved self-image are important subgoals of such a programme, not merely accidental byproducts.

This was an excellent programme, but it was not an exceptional one. Rather, it is typical of many such programmes which workers have had the opportunity to set up with us because they were following in-service training. The enthusiasm of participants and the progress they have been able to achieve strongly suggest that there is scope for much more work to be done in this setting if only the resources are made available in terms of staff time and appropriate training input and support.

A GROUP PROGRAMME FOCUSING ON INDIVIDUAL PROBLEMS

In the second unit, a joint programme of work was carried out by Pete and Jim, who were both completing in-service professional training. Pete was an instructor with a craft background in the day centre itself, while Jim was a physiology graduate working in the adjoining residential hostel. The two were firm friends and this fact, together with the complementary nature of their background and personality, probably contributed a lot to making the programme such a successful one. It differs in emphasis from that described above in that, while there was an element of work on difficulties experienced in common by group members, there was an unusually large element of individuality built into it. Pete and Jim selected the clients for the group after considerable discussion, and each of them supplemented the group programme by some further skills training with one client on an individual basis.

As they were designing the programme, Pete and Jim reflected on the limited learning opportunities which the day centre offered. Pete commented on the lack of appropriate models for clients, who were surrounded by numbers of people actually modelling inappropriate, maladaptive or immature behaviour. He recognized how important it is for professional carers to be aware of their potential influence as models of appropriate and socially acceptable behaviour and a particularly notable facet of the work with this group was the very effective modelling which the leaders offered.

The group comprised three young men and three girls with mild to moderate mental handicap; all could communicate quite well orally, though two of them had specific problems, one a cleft palate and the other a mild stutter. The additional sessions were carried out with Mike, a young man who was having problems in his relationship with his father, and Sheila, a young woman with a morbid fear of police officers. Both of these problems were deemed to be suitable for work in the group setting as well, since the clients concerned welcomed the idea and there was enough that was familiar to other members in these situations for them to be of general interest.

The group work was planned around 10 45-minute sessions made up of a short initial discussion followed by a period of coaching, modelling and prompted role-play; video was introduced at an early stage and the members took to it very readily. Individual sessions were slotted in between meetings and comprised six sessions with Mike and 13 with Sheila. Group sessions were later extended by 15 minutes to make a full hour.

The First Five Group Sessions

The first session began with a welcome and introduction to the group and this led on to a simple role-play on asking a stranger the way to the toilet, designed to illustrate the method which would be used. Pete and Jim went on to explain some more what the group was about and stressed that membership was voluntary. There followed a short discussion about non-verbal behaviour and how it can express feelings. One leader modelled some facial expressions, which the members then imitated, the leaders drawing attention to how it felt to make a particular kind of face. They went on to do simple voice exercises to illustrate that "It's not always what you say that counts, but the way you say it". A number of very short exercises on this theme were accompanied by generous social reinforcement of the participants. In general the members were most enthusiastic about this opening session, the only hesitation being expressed by one member who had found some of the language used rather hard to follow. The leaders took due note of this and made a firm resolve to be more careful about use of jargon in the future. Accordingly, there were no further problems of this kind.

The second meeting began with a resume of what had been done at the previous one and a clear and explicit restatement of the contract, viz: 10 sessions of 45 minutes on Wednesday and Thursday mornings. The leaders acted out some more role-plays then drew in members and started together with them to establish some assignments—things group members could agree to do before they met again the following week. Exercises demonstrating the importance of eye contact and posture were followed by some simple role-plays of greeting visitors to the centre and taking them to a workshop. The element of fun and enjoyment was highlighted during this session, so too was the confidentiality aspect—"You mustn't gossip to people outside the group about what you see people doing there". The clients clearly enjoyed the session enormously and would have liked to go on longer with the role-plays, so it was at this point the leaders decided to renegotiate the time element in the programme and have sessions of a full hour's duration.

The following week began with a recap of session two and confirmation that hour-long sessions had been agreed. The previous input on posture and eye contact was repeated and elaborated and the confidentiality aspect was highlighted again. Pete and Jim then quickly moved the group on to more role-plays, this time using a variety of kinds of greeting. The following situations were all modelled first by the leaders:

- Greeting a visitor to the centre
- Brief greeting to an acquaintance in the street
- Affectionate greeting to a relation or close friend

After appropriate reinforcement, the group moved on to a brainstorming session to determine what were the areas on which members most wished to work. The following order of preference emerged:

- Fear of policemen
- Dealing with aggression
- Talking to the opposite sex
- Avoiding rows with parents
- Taking problems to staff
- Coping with noisy people
- Approaching people in shops and similar settings

By this time, the group were clearly showing a good understanding of the method and the kinds of things it could achieve. The brainstorming, after a rather slow start, eventually produced a series of very good suggestions, role-playing had become easier and there was a good understanding and acceptance of the need for confidentiality.

Next day's session began as usual with reminders of the previous day's work and the ideas which had emerged from the brainstorm. Pete and Jim began desensitizing group members to police officers by handing round a policeman's helmet which members proceeded to put on, to the accompaniment of a good deal of laughter (itself an excellent counter to anxiety). Without dwelling too long on this topic, they moved on to everyday scenes which might occur at the hostel and the centre, for instance:

- "I've forgotten my dinner money" (to staff at centre)
- "I don't want to go home this weekend" (at hostel)

One member, Kath, had previously mentioned a problem with her mother; this was explored very gently and she role-played it with the study supervisor for Pete and Jim, whom the group already knew. Several more role-plays followed of very straightforward situations involving policemen such as asking for directions. The leaders modelled each of these before coaching and prompting members to follow suit, taking care to reinforce them warmly for achieving something about which they had felt a great deal of anxiety. For the first time some simple homework tasks were agreed at the end of the meeting.

Next week, the fifth session began with the replaying of some of the video film made the previous week. Kath said she was sorry she hadn't completed her homework task, but a suitable opportunity had simply not arisen; other members whose tasks were less dependent on circumstances had mostly completed theirs. There was some further brainstorming, which produced some more possible problem areas for work. The "policeman" role-play was developed further, this time with a leader wearing the policeman's helmet. Mike now mentioned that he would like to be able to go to the station and buy a Saver ticket to take him to London, and this too was systematically modelled and then performed with the necessary degree of coaching and prompting. Mike was quite anxious about it, so sequences were kept very short so as to leave him with a positive feeling about his progress. Group members asked towards the end whether sessions could be extended further to one and a quarter hours, as there was so much they wanted to do. By this stage they had improved a lot in giving each other reinforcement and they had made a start on generalizing their learning through homework tasks but this needed more time to develop.

Individual Work with Two Members of the Group

The work with Sheila continued throughout the programme, concentrating on desensitizing her to police officers and to interaction with them. Pete obtained the help of a neighbour of his, Denis, who was a serving police officer, was very keen to participate and in fact played a major part in the programme. During the first individual session with Sheila, Pete established some factual details about her fear of policemen, the degree of anxiety she experienced, the circumstances in which it manifested itself and the way it had developed.

On occasions she would try to avoid policemen in the street, sometimes even running away and hiding from them. She had an uncle living in the north of England who was a policeman and about whom she felt quite anxious, so that on her last visit there she had run away and hidden when she saw him in his uniform. Her fears seemed to have developed since she left school and to have been exacerbated by seeing television film of police "fighting" in disturbances with striking miners and also of police "fighting" at football matches. About four years ago there had been a spate of thefts from the centre, and the consequent police enquiries had increased her anxiety further.

Pete sketched out an initial programme for work with Sheila based on the following graded stages:

1. Obtaining an illustrated booklet about the force from the local police which she and Pete could look at together
2. Role-play with Sheila's boy-friend playing the part of a policeman (this was a very simple "enquiry" role-play)
3. Doing the same role-play with another group member
4. Repeating it with the centre manager (an ex-policeman)
5. Repeating it with Denis (the real policeman) in civilian clothes
6. Finally, performing the role-play with Denis in his uniform

The sessions were short and frequent, with maximum periods of 30 minutes, several times a week. It soon emerged that Sheila found the police helmet particularly intimidating, so Pete made a great deal of use of the helmet he had borrowed, thereby enabling Sheila to overcome her fears about it. The 13 sessions with Sheila employed the usual methods of guided role-play, together with the booklet and the helmet, and culminated with Sheila's twenty-third role-play in which she addressed the policeman in full uniform, putting a series of several questions to him in the car-park adjoining the centre. This interchange was filmed by the two workers from inside the centre and offers ample evidence not only of Sheila's achievement but also her delight and pride in her newly developed ability.

The work with Mike on developing more independence and more assertive patterns of behaviour was conducted along similar lines, and though it was rather less dramatic it did result in a much improved level of performance and also in an increase in his general level of confidence. One particularly useful device which he learned to adopt was "broken record", that is, the response of simply repeating in the same words what you want to say without allowing yourself to be disarmed or sidetracked by the other party who is trying to persuade or manipulate you. Mike developed a good capacity to use this simple but effective device.

To monitor and record the progress these clients made, the two workers used a rating scale on social interaction which features the following items: posture, movement, proximity, touch, eye contact, speech content and speech quality. They noted significant improvements under all the headings except touch, which did not feature in the programme.

Meanwhile the group continued to meet for the projected total of 10 sessions along similar lines to the initial ones, and it was noticeable that not only did they make progress on the specific items they had themselves pinpointed but their general social behaviour displayed the same kind of development, so that they were viewed more favourably by others in the centre and the hostel and were able to feel more positive and confident.

FEATURES EMERGING FROM THE WORK WITH MENTALLY HANDICAPPED CLIENTS

The clients in these studies, as in fact in all the work with mentally handicapped clients to which we have contributed, were most enthusiastic about their programmes so that motivation was never a problem. Ironically, perhaps, it is often other staff who raise objections and difficulties and make gloomy prognostications about the clients' capacity to learn. If, however, colleagues do understand and believe in the method, they can often be encouraged to participate as well as give general support and this can be a tremendous asset: one of the striking features of the work by Pete and Jim was the way they brought in additional participants to some of the work (study supervisor, centre manager and policeman). By doing this it is possible to avoid the sharp break which can be experienced between practice in the training sessions and in the actual, real-life situation, so that generalization of what is being learned becomes a smooth, continuous process.

In these studies the workers were adept at maintaining the interest and motivation of group members; an element of "entertainment" was never absent from the sessions. Of course, video is in itself associated with entertainment, and in addition workers running groups for mentally handicapped clients often lean heavily on the use of games, especially ones chosen to foster interaction and trust. Moreover, the situations chosen for role-play often include an element of fantasy: a group of people with moderate handicap from a hostel chose to role-play with us a royal reception in which they took the parts of queen and princesses as well as of those meeting them. Despite the "make-believe" element, they were still learning about important aspects of social behaviour such as speech, posture and eye contact.

This client involvement in choices about the work that was to be done is an impressive feature of both these projects. In particular, much of the initial assessment work was a joint undertaking: checklists and brainstorming were both very effective at identifying problems to be worked on. Of course, this has the disadvantage that people may have problems of which they are not aware and which will therefore not emerge, though they may do so at a slightly later stage if devices like reverse role-plays or video are used. Insofar as professional judgements and agency records make a contribution to the assessment, these are only useful if they refer to the current situation and recent observations. Use of old material such as assessment sheets or test scores dating from a year or more ago when the client first came to the agency may actually do more harm than good.

The extent to which the clients can share in the responsibility for selecting targets and planning the programme can come as a surprise to some staff members, who may tend to be pessimistic about clients' capacities and complacent about what is already offered to them. Equally, the rate of progress made in programmes of this kind is sometimes little short of amazing and suggests that many mentally handicapped people have severely deficient social skills simply through lack of awareness and the failure of others in their environment to give them any feedback. Very little has been expected of them in the past, and nothing demanded, which amounts to acceptance not only of the underlying mental handicap but also of the socially constructed handicap which overlies it. Acceptance of this kind of social handicap is no kindness to the persons concerned, whose need is rather for help in identifying excesses or deficits in their behaviour together with specific ways of improving it. These are the familiar techniques of guided role-play, especially modelling and the use of video, and above all the opportunity to practise in a safe, secure atmosphere—and a great deal of warm, approving response from the leaders. The work described in this chapter in fact used this social approval (from leaders and other group members) as almost the only form of reinforcement, since the clients responded so well to it and valued it so highly.

> As an example of quite remarkably fast progress with minimal rein-
> forcement we might cite Fred, a very tall young man attending a day
> centre who habitually stood very close to people when talking to them.
> This would have been experienced as quite uncomfortable anyway, but
> the effect was increased by his height, so that it actually seemed quite
> threatening although he was not a particularly aggressive young man.
> After only one session, with the help of video replay, Fred was able to
> see the effect which this closeness had on other people and immediately
> began to modify his approach both in a social skills group and outside
> it, so that staff members were struck by the way he immediately started
> to make adjustments in the way he approached them.

Although they may not at the outset anticipate such a success, staff who have experience of working with mentally handicapped clients and a commitment to enriching their lives and enhancing their capacities are usually well equipped to undertake programmes of this kind, given some initial help in starting to design them and support in the execution. They may be surprised by what they achieve. Because they know their clients so well, they will have the knowledge to decide how to approach asking clients to undertake things, how to sequence role-plays, how to give feedback without undermining and, in fact, all the skills required for the execution of the programmes. What they do need is continuing support, sugges-tions on a take-it-or-leave-it basis, and possibly the opportunity to try out some approaches in a simulation with peers. Two workers who were just starting a group were concerned that one of the members frequently acted in a noisy and attention-seeking way which they feared might disrupt group sessions entirely. The tutors' advice was to give him a clear role in helping another group member in his own role-play. The whole group of tutors and workers then simulated part of a session in which the two workers as group leaders could experiment with doing this. Not surprisingly perhaps, this worked well in the simulation, but as tutors we could not be sure how effective it would prove *in vivo*. We were therefore very relieved to hear that the approach had been most successful, there having been no sign whatever of the anticipated problems of disruptive behaviour.

We have stressed throughout this book, and perhaps most of all in this chapter, that social skills training is essentially an individualized, "custom-built" approach to helping which relies heavily on client participation. While the method has some affinities with behaviour therapy, as is shown most clearly in the work on fear of contact with policemen, and while quite clear-cut practical techniques are involved, it remains true that its essential quality is that it is caring, helping and empowering.

REFERENCES

Alberti, R.E. and Emmons M.L. (1970). *Your Perfect Right.* Impact.

Argyle, M. (ed.) (1981). *Social Skills and Work.* Methuen.

Barclay Committee (1982). *Social Workers: Their Role and Task.* Bedford Square Press.

Bartlett, H. (1970). *The Common Base of Social Work Practice.* New York, National Association of Social Workers, Inc.

Batten, T.R. (1967). *The Non-Directive Approach in Group and Community Work.* Oxford University Press.

Berne, E. (1968). *Games People Play.* Penguin.

Biestek, F.P. (1961). *The Casework Relationship.* Allen and Unwin.

Brager, G. and Specht, H. (1973). *Community Organising.* Columbia University Press.

Brewer, C. and Laite, J. (1980). *Can Social Work Survive?* Smith.

Briscoe, C. and Thomas, D. (eds) (1977). *Community Work: Learning and Supervision.* George Allen & Unwin.

Butler, B. and Elliott, D. (1985). *Teaching and Learning for Practice.* Gower.

Butrym, Z. (1976). *The Nature of Social Work.* Macmillan.

Calouste Gulbenkian Foundation (1968). *Community Work and Social Change: A Report on Training.* Longmans.

Chapman, E.K. (1978). *Visually Handicapped Children and Young People.* Routledge & Kegan Paul.

Clement, P. and Milne, P. (1967). Group play therapy and tangible reinforcers used to modify the behavior of 8-year-old boys. *Behavior Research and Therapy,* no. 5.

Clough, R. (1981). *Old Age Homes.* NISW/Allen & Unwin.

Collins, M. (1981). From role-play to reality. *Community Care,* 17 September.

Collins, J. and Collins, M. (1981). *Achieving Change in Social Work.* Heinemann.

Danbury, H. (1979/1985). *Teaching Practical Social Work.* Bedford Square Press/Heinemann.

Davies, M. (1981/1985). *The Essential Social Worker.* Heinemann.

Davis, L. (1982). *Residential Care: A Community Resource.* Heinemann.

Douglas, R. and Payne, C. (1987). *Learning about Caring.* NISW/Allen & Unwin.

Egan, G. (1975, 1982, 1986, 1990). *The Skilled Helper.* Brooks/Cole.

Ellis, R.A.F. and Whittington, D. (1981). *A Guide to Social Skill Training.* Croom Helm.

Epstein, H. (1975). In H. Jones, (ed.), *Towards a New Social Work.* Routledge & Kegan Paul.

Epting, F.R. (1984). *Personal Construct Counseling and Psychotherapy.* Wiley.

Fischer, J. (1976). *The Effectiveness of Social Casework.* Thomas.

Fisher, R. and Ury, W. (1981). *Getting to Yes.* Hutchinson Business.

Goldberg, A.M. (1970). *Helping the Aged.* Allen & Unwin.

Goldberg, A.M. and Warburton, R. (1979). *Ends and Means in Social Work.* Allen & Unwin.

Goldstein, H. (1973). *Social Work Practice: A Unitary Approach.* University of South Carolina Press.

Haines, J. (1975). *Skills and Methods in Social Work.* Constable.

Hallett, C. and Stevenson, O. (1980). *Child Abuse: Aspects of Interprofessional Co-operation.* Allen & Unwin.

Hargie, O., Saunders, C. and Dickson, D. (1981). *Social Skills in Interpersonal Communication.* Croom Helm.

Henderson, P. and Thomas, D. (1980). *Skills in Neighbourhood Work.* NISW/Allen & Unwin.

Hollin, C.R. and Trower, P. (1986). *Handbook of Social Skills Training.* Pergamon.

Hollis, F. (1956). *Casework: A Psychosocial Therapy.* Random House.

Holmes, B. and Bryant, R. (1977). *Fieldwork teaching in community work.* In C. Briscoe and D. Thomas (eds), *Community Work: Learning and Supervision.* George Allen & Unwin.

Jehu, D., Hardiker, P., Yelloly, M. and Shaw, M. (1972). *Behaviour Modification in Social Work.* Wiley.

Jones, H. (ed.) (1975). *Towards a New Social Work.* Routledge & Kegan Paul.

Jordan, B. (1973). *Paupers.* Routledge & Kegan Paul.

Kadushin, A. (1973, 1983). *The Social Work Interview.* Columbia University Press.

Keith-Lucas, A. (1972). *Giving and Taking Help.* Chapel Hill.

Laing, R.D. and Esterson, A. (1964). *Sanity, Madness and the Family.* Tavistock.

Lazarus, A.A. (1971). *Behavior Therapy and Beyond.* McGraw Hill.

Lazarus, A.A. (ed.) (1976). *Multi-Modal Behavior Therapy.* McGraw Hill.

Leonard, P. (1975). In R. Bailey and M. Brake, (eds), *Radical Social Work.* Edward Arnold.

Liberman, R.P., King, L.W., De Risi, W.J. and McCann, M. (1975). *Personal Effectiveness.* Research Press.

Lishman, J. (1978). A Clash in Perspective? A Study of Worker and Client Perceptions of Social Work. *British Journal of Social Work,* 8, 301–311.

Matson, J.L. and Ollendick, T.H. (1988). *Enhancing Children's Social Skills: Assessment and Training.* Pergamon.

Mattinson, J. (1975). *The Reflection Process in Casework Supervision.* Tavistock.

Mattinson, J. and Sinclair, I. (1979). *Mate and Stalemate: Working with Marital Problems in a Social Service Department.* Blackwell.

Mayer, J. and Timms, N. (1970). *The Client Speaks.* Routledge & Kegan Paul.

Meichenbaum, D. (1977). *Cognitive-Behavior Modification: An Integrative Approach.* Plenum Press.

Miller, E.J. and Gwynne, G.V. (1972). *A Life Apart.* Tavistock.

Nelson-Jones, R. (1983). *Practical Counselling Skills.* Holt Rinehart & Winston.

Oster, G.D., Caro, J.E., Eagen, D.R. and Lillo, M.A. (1988). *Assessing Adolescents.* Pergamon.

Parsloe, P. (1981). *Social Services Area Teams.* Allen & Unwin.

Perry, F.G. (1982). The relationship between the qualifying training and the work of the probation officer. MA Thesis, Keele University.

Phelps, N. and Austin, N. (1975). *The Assertive Woman.* Impact.

Pincus, A. and Minahan, A. (1973). *Social Work Practice: Model and Method.* Peacock.

Priestley, P., McGuire, J., Flegg, D., Hemsley, V. and Welham, D. (1978). *Social Skills and Personal Problem-Solving.* Tavistock.

Priestley, P. and McGuire, J. (1983). *Learning to Help.* Tavistock.

Priestley, P., McGuire, J., Flegg, D., Hemsley, V., Welham, D. and Barnitt, R. (1984). *Social Skills in Prison and the Community.* Routledge and Kegan Paul.

Rackham, N. et al (1971) (eds). *Developing Interactive Skills*. Wellens.

Rachman, S. (1971). *The Effects of Psychotherapy*. Pergamon.

Rees, S. and Wallace, A. (1982). *Verdicts on Social Work*. Edward Arnold.

Reid, W.J. and Epstein, L. (1972). *Task-Centered Casework*. Columbia University Press.

Rogers, C. (1942). *Counseling and Psychotherapy*. Houghton Mifflin.

Rose, S.D. (1972). *Treating Children in Groups*. Jossey-Bass.

Rosenhan, D.L. (1973). On being sane in insane places. *Science*, no. 179.

Sainsbury, E., Nixon, S. and Phillips, D. (1982). *Social Work in Focus*. Routledge and Kegan Paul.

Sainsbury, E. (1975). *Social Work with Families*. Routledge and Kegan Paul.

Seligman, M. (1975). *Helplessness: On Depression, Development and Death*. W.H. Freeman.

Simpkin, M. (1978). *Trapped Within Welfare*. Macmillan.

Sinclair, I. (1971). *Hostels for Probationers*. HMSO.

Sinclair, I. (1988). *Residential Care: The Research Reviewed*. NISW/HMSO.

Smith, M.J. (1975). *When I Say No, I Feel Guilty*. Bantam.

Specht, H. and Vickery, A. (eds) (1977). *Integrating Social Work Methods*. NISW/Allen & Unwin.

Timms, N. (1972). *Recording in Social Work*. Routledge & Kegan Paul.

Trower, P. (ed.) (1984). *Radical Approaches to Social Skills Training*. Croom Helm.

Trower, P., Bryant, B. and Argyle, M. (1978). *Social Skills and Mental Health*. Methuen.

Truax, C.B. and Carkhuff, R.R. (1967). *Towards Effective Counseling and Psychotherapy*. Aldine.

Twelvetrees, A. (1982). *Community Work*. Macmillan.

Wagner Report (1988). *Residential Care: A Positive Choice*. NISW/HMSO.

Warnock Report (1978). *Special Educational Needs*. HMSO.

Wilkinson, J. and Canter, S. (1982). *Social Skills Training Manual*. Wiley.

Wootton, B. (1959). *Social Science and Social Pathology*. Allen and Unwin.

Wright, D. (1979). *The Social Worker and the Courts*. Heinemann.

Wynne, G. et al (1987). Inability of trained nurses to perform basic life support. *British Medical Journal*, **294**, 1198–1199.

Yelloly, M. (1980). *Social Work Theory and Psychoanalysis*. Van Nostrand Reinhold.

INDEX